Wisconsin's Statewide Guide to Stand Up Paddleboarding

Ben Shaw

D1378125

BOULDER

Published by Trails Books
a Big Earth Publishing company
3005 Center Green Drive, Suite 225
Boulder, Colorado 80301
1-800-258-5830
E-mail: books@bigearthpublishing.com
www.bigearthpublishing.com

Cover and text design by D.K. Luraas
ISBN: 978-1-934553-43-5

Library of Congress Cataloging-in-Publication Data on file

9   8   7   6   5   4   3   2   1

Printed in the United States of America

In Memory of Jim Hudson

Contents

Acknowledgments

I'd like to thank my wife Joon for her loving, proactive support, patience, proofreading, and co-piloting many of our scouting missions. She is both a wonder and a force of nature. And, thank you Lindsay Wood Davis for your freely and frequently given advice, expansive knowledge and understanding of Wisconsin's waterways and culture. Your guidance has been absolutely instrumental to this work. You're a gentleman, a scholar, and a heck of an uncle! Thanks Mark Cupp at Lower Wisconsin State Riverway Board and John Elliot at Friends of the Black River for your input. Thanks to the countless folks who have helped with info and insight on and off the water and over the web. And yes, NooRoongGi, we will be going for a walk soon.

Introduction

Welcome to the *Wisconsin Statewide Guide to Stand Up Paddleboarding*. We're beaming that you've cracked the book and are interested in SUP here in Wisconsin. Stand up paddleboarding is a juggernaut. It is easily the fastest growing water sport in the USA. Resurrected from its ancient Hawaiian roots by surfers like Laird Hamilton, Dave Kalama, and Rick Thomas, SUP is exploding in the Midwest. It's easy to learn, a great workout, and is one style of surfing that doesn't require a coast. Actually, it is perfectly suited to the water trails of Wisconsin. From the Lake Michigan shoreline to the Mississippi River, and north to Lake Superior, people are "Hanging 10" and getting in shape. They are also experiencing the nature that this state has to offer from a totally new perspective. Try some yoga on Lake Wingra, paddle over submerged pyramids on Rock Lake, glide down the twisting Pecatonica or brave the Sea Caves of the Apostle Islands. Come and join us as we explore fifty trips and SUP sweet spots that are downright the best here in Wisconsin.

This fun guide features an easy-to-use water finder, tons of pictures, close to ninety handy QR code links to put-ins and take-outs for your smartphone, descriptions of water features en-route, and a concise technique section to get you up and gliding. The book is laid out by region and water type. Simply open to a section of the state that you are interested in exploring and then jump to your choice of Flatwater Classics (lakes), River Sessions (rivers), or the Third Coast (Great Lakes).

We hope that this book can introduce more people to the wonderful waterways in this great state. They offer us solitude, companionship, community, and better health, environment, and economies. They have so much to offer and are in need of all the stewards who will answer the call. Paddlers of every stripe must take an active role in protecting, preserving, and conserving Wisconsin's bodies of water. To get you in the spirit, we've listed a classic surf song that aurally describes each spot.

QR Codes

We chose to include QR Codes in this book because they are an easy way to connect you with where you are going. Every time you scan a link from this book, it will pinpoint the spot you are reading about in Google Maps. From there you will be able to get exact, turn-by-turn driving directions to the launch site. QR stands for Quick Response and is simply a different style of barcode. They were originally developed by Toyota to track inventory, but they are a very handy way of "clicking" on a printed link. All you need is a smartphone and a QR scanning app. For the Apple iPhone, we recommend QR Reader for iPhone, Scan, or Red Laser. And for Android/Google Play, we recommend QR Droid, Red Laser, or QR Barcode Scanner Pro. Generally, you only need to start the app, and hold it steadily over the page. When the app recognizes the barcode, it will ask you what you would like to do with the information. Choose "Open Link" and your phone's screen will be taken to Google Maps. For those of you who do not have a smartphone, we have listed easy-to-use short Internet links to the locations. Who said nature and technology don't mix? Not us!

Leave No Trace

In an effort to maximize stand up paddleboarding's positive effect on you, consider acting in the best interest of the environment that you enjoy this sport in. Here are the Seven Principles of "Leave No Trace" published by The Leave No Trace Center for Outdoor Ethics. We encourage you to incorporate these simple steps into your time enjoying nature. Human impact on nature is inevitable. To what extent, negative or positive, begins with you.

Plan Ahead and Prepare
- Learn about river-specific issues, regulations, and permits
- Use a river guidebook and map to plan your trip
- Schedule your trip so that you encounter appropriate river flows for your group's ability
- Repackage food to minimize waste
- Know river skills and carry the necessary equipment to minimize your impact

Travel and Camp on Durable Surfaces
- Durable surfaces include rock, gravel, and sand
- Focus activity where vegetation is absent
- Concentrate use on existing trails and campsites
- Select a campsite large enough for your group
- When on day hikes in the river corridor, walk single file in the middle of the trail, even when muddy
- In pristine areas, disperse uses to prevent creation of new campsites and trails
- Leave campsites clean and natural looking

Dispose of Waste Properly
- Pack it in, pack it out
- Use a washable, reusable toilet or other approved method to pack out human waste, toilet paper, and tampons. Check local regulations for requirements and recommended procedures.
- Liquid wastes can be dumped into the main current in many high-volume (over 500 CFS) rivers. In low-volume rivers, scat-

ter liquid waste 200 feet from water, away from camps and trails. Check local regulations.
- Urinating directly into the river is often the best option. Check local regulations.
- Use a tarp in the camp kitchen to catch food and trash, which attract unwanted animals.
- Pack out all small food particles and small pieces of trash.

Leave What You Find
- Appreciate ancient structures, artifacts, rock art, and other natural objects, but leave them undisturbed
- Do not build structures or dig trenches in campsites
- Avoid introducing non-native species, including live bait, by cleaning equipment between trips

Minimize Campfire Impacts
- Minimize campfire impacts by using stoves
- Use a fire pan or designated fire ring for open fires and charcoal
- Elevate fire pan and use a blanket to catch embers
- Use dead and downed wood no larger than an adults wrist to keep the fire small
- Consider bringing your own firewood or charcoal
- Burn all wood and charcoal to ash. Carry out ash with other garbage.

Respect Wildlife
- Observe wildlife from a distance. Do not follow or approach them.
- Never feed wildlife, as it damages their health, alters natural behaviors, and exposes them to predators and other dangers.
- Protect wildlife by storing food and trash securely
- Control pets or leave them behind
- Avoid wildlife during sensitive times: mating, nesting, or when food is scarce.

Be Considerate of Other Visitors
- Respect other visitors and protect the quality of their experience

- Communicate with other river visitors about your floating and camping plans
- Leave larger camps for larger groups
- Avoid camping or eating near major rapids where scouting and portaging take place
- Non-motorized crafts usually have the right-of-way over powerboats; slower boats should keep to the right
- Let nature's sounds prevail

The member-driven Leave No Trace Center for Outdoor Ethics teaches people how to enjoy the outdoors responsibly. This copyrighted information has been reprinted with permission from the Leave No Trace Center for Outdoor Ethics: *www.LNT.org*. For more information about how you can become involved in conserving Wisconsin's Waterways, contact the River Alliance of Wisconsin at (608) 257-2424, or visit them at *www.wisconsinrivers.org/*.

How To SUP

Are you breathing? Check. Can you stand on a sidewalk? Check. There, we've covered the primary requirements! You make an excellent candidate for SUP glory. Stand up paddleboarding is a high success rate sport. It's not that you won't find it a little challenging; it's more that you'll have the hang of it quickly. Moreover, you'll be hooked. Give it a try and you'll find that you can maneuver with confidence in no time flat. While we are not aiming to provide the definitive guide to this great sport, the instructions that follow will provide an excellent primer to get you on the water.

First, let us don our Mom hat for a moment with a word on safety. Know and accept your swimming abilities and cardiovascular condition. Don't bite off more than you can chew. Always wear a life vest and if it comes to it, choose the board over your paddle. Given the choice, always begin your session upwind. It will make getting back to your starting point without running out of steam much easier.

How To Stand Up

Find a spot with calm, flat water (and preferably with somebody you enjoy laughing with) for your first outing. Put the board in water that is deep enough for the fin to float freely. We generally start in lake water that is knee to thigh deep. Start out kneeling in the middle of the board and take a couple of strokes on each side of the board. After you're comfortable in the kneeling position, slowly and fluidly stand up, one foot after another. It helps to hold the paddle perpendicularly on the board as you stand, so that you don't fumble with it after you're up. Stay in the middle of the board with knees slightly bent and with your feet parallel and shoulder width apart.

The first time you stand, you might find the board feels wobbly or tippy. This gets better with practice. If you need to reposition your feet, think baby steps. You will tend to stiffen up, so relax and try to stay loose. Your paddle is your chum. Use it to balance like a tightrope walker might use his pole. Finding balance in this sport is much like many other board sports, it becomes much easier with sustained forward momentum. One last point—Did you know the Hawaiian word for stand is 'ku'?

How to Paddle

Once you have stood up, grip the top of the paddle in one hand as if it were a cap and then grip the middle of the paddle with the other hand. Keep your mitts at least shoulder width apart or the power of your stroke will be diminished. Your lower hand and arm will remain relatively stable while your top hand will act as if pushing a lever. Believe it or not, paddling an SUP is more about moving your core than arm movement. Allow the compression of your trunk to guide the stroke. Try to picture your paddle as pulling the board forward in the water. Start the stroke as far forward on the board as you are comfortable with and dip the blade fully into the water before starting the stroke.

Don't continue the stroke too far past your legs, because if you continue the stroke as you would a canoe stroke, the paddle actually creates some turbulence that makes tracking and forward progress more difficult. Try stroking a few times on the right and then a few on the left. Switching sides can help you to maintain a straight direction. This is called tracking. The better you become, the less and less you will need to switch sides, but it is perfectly acceptable to change sides as needed.

How to Turn Around

Your primary means of turning around will initially be by something called the C Stroke. Largely the same as its canoeing cousin, the C Stroke is executed by starting your blade at the tail of the board and pull the paddle toward the tip in an arch while twisting your core. Conversely, the C Stroke can just as effectively be used from the tip of the SUP to turn the opposite direction.

And there you have it! You can now stand up and paddle and turn back to where you came from. Now all that stands between you and serene SUP glory is practice, practice, practice.

How to SUP with Fido

We love our dogs and we love spending time outside with them even more, right? Many people love getting out on the water with their beloved pet. Here are a few basics to help introduce the sport to your favorite four-legged companion. Help the dog into its own personal flotation device (PFD). Even if Fido is a good swimmer, you will appreciate the handle later. Keep the session short and positive. Also make sure the deck on your paddleboard has a nice traction area. A slick deck can make for a tough time. Give your dog plenty of time to get used to the board and paddle. Begin training Fido to get on and off the board on dry land. Only move to the water when Fido is comfortable getting on and staying on the SUP. When you do take the show down to the water, let Fido get on the board and get used to it before you push off. When you mount the board, make sure the dog stays in front of you and that you begin in the kneeling position. And don't forget the praise and treats!

Note, no dog is going to be comfortable or calm without its caregiver being stone-cold confident. A negative first outing may turn off even a hearty water dog.

**How to
stand up**

**How to
stand up**

How to stand up

How to paddle

How to SUP with Fido

Aaron Peterson/aaronpeterson.net

Section Descriptions

Flatwater Classics

It would be easy to spend a lifetime exploring Wisconsin's 15,000-plus lakes. Fall in love with the many peaceful, clear, sandy-bottom bodies of water on your paddleboard.

Try out SUP yoga at Lake Wingra, splash around a bustling summer beach scene in Lake Geneva, hang ten over ancient pyramids at Rock Lake, or simply take a deep breath and enjoy gliding through a sunny afternoon exploring the many bays, inlets, and islands that these marvelous inland lakes have to offer.

The lakes we've selected are the absolute best SUP spots that Wisconsin has to offer. These are also the ideal place to begin your SUP experience. Paddle around, work on your balance, take your kid or dog (or both!) out for some epic "Flatwater Classic" fun.

River Sessions

The Badger State's 12,600 rivers and streams flow over 84,000 miles of the state's scenic and varied terrain. Wisconsin loves water recreation and the SUP phenom is spreading quickly. The state's progressive water trails system provides a network of access points, resting places, and attractions for paddlers. Some trails are interpretive routes, some usher paddlers up to campsites, and some even connect communities. From relaxing sunny floats to exhilarating riffles and even a few rapids, Wisconsin's rivers provide ample opportunity to further enjoy this wondrous sport. The sections and segments we recommend in this guide are geared toward intermediate to advanced SUPers. Even at full skill level, SUPs tend to move a little slower in the water so we've deliberately chosen shorter, less technical sections of these superlative waterways. It's time to experience these state treasures in a whole new way!

Only attempt running river SUP after you have become sure-footed, agile on flat water, and very comfortable with your equipment. River hazards can be as subtle as they are strong. Always let someone know where you are going. Always surf a river with a companion; never wear a leash, which can become entangled on fallen trees; and always peel out (portage) to scope riffly or rapid sections. It is also recommended that you run rivers with inflatable boards, or "iSUPs." They are made from the same materials as whitewater rafts and will bounce off of rocks. They are also not as prone to damage from scraping the river bottom.

Third Coast

Wisconsin is lucky enough to border not one, but two of the Great Lakes. These gargantuan bodies of water grace the state with over 1,100 miles of scenic coastline. Whether you are look-ing for a natural experience on a solitary windswept beach or would rather mix it up at an urban beach, Wisconsin's coast of-fers something for everyone. Push out on an SUP and experi-ence these beautiful bodies of water in a whole new way.

The third coast has long had a healthy surf culture. Many of those crazy enough to suit up and head in during the winter months fill the ranks of the Badger State's SUP community, but this section's intention is on relatively calm places for SUP. We won't be giving out anybody's secret spots—well maybe one or two! We recommend places where you can have a reliably good day when the wind is down.

Come check out all the crazy sweet spots that Chequamegon Bay in Lake Superior has to offer. Quietly slip out for a dawn patrol at one of the Big Bay Parks on Madeline Island. Or hit Lake Michigan and chill in between sessions at a full service cabana at Bradford Beach in Milwaukee. Wisconsin has so many good beaches you'll wonder why you ever started California Dreamin' in the first place. Oh right … winter … but you get the point, right?

Speaking of weather, it can and does change quickly on these lakes. The lake occasionally becomes too hazardous even for very large boats. Check forecasts before leaving for the day. Let someone know where you are headed and paddle with a buddy or two. On Lake Superior, keep an eye to the west and southwest for incoming weather. It will give you the opportunity to whisper "something wicked this way comes" in your best sailor's brogue before paddling back to your launch safely. Never set out in fog. You can get turned around quite easily and larger vessels will not see you. Remember to always wear a PFD and dress for getting wet. Hypothermia is real and escalates very quickly. You might find that a pair of wetsuit booties makes an SUP session on these magnificent lakes just that much better.

So strap those boards to a car, throw our guidebook in the back seat and gear up for a cheese-curd and Sprecher-fueled Surf Safari!

Wisconsin

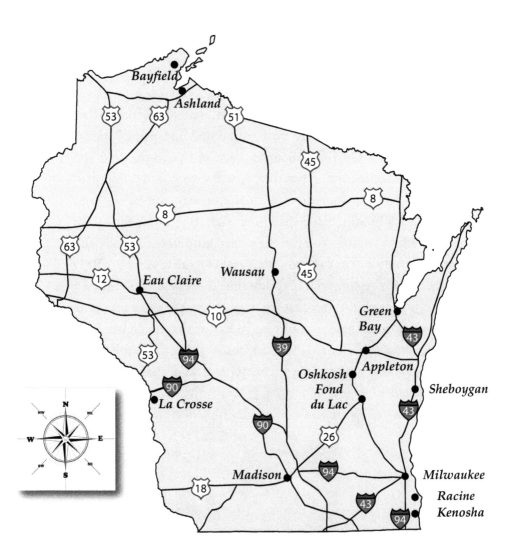

Southwest
Wisconsin

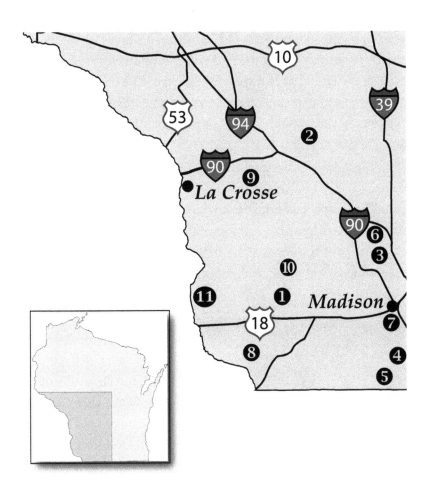

SW Flatwater Classics

I. Blackhawk Lake

Blackhawk Lake is situated in the rolling hills of southern Wisconsin, about an hour west of Madison. This lake is perfect for a sunny, summer afternoon SUP session. Blackhawk is a 220-acre, man-made lake that is never deeper than 40 feet. Even though gas-powered boats are allowed on the lake, there is a strict No Wake policy, so you'll be sure to paddle peacefully on any day you choose to visit.

You can launch your board from the sandy beach or the paved, public boat launch. Park entrance fee is $6 for a daily pass. Bring a packed lunch and while away some hours. The recreation area offers great camping spots and picnic shelters. The campsites are roomy and the bathrooms and showers are well maintained. Sites are $12 per night. Call (608) 623-2707 for more information.

From Madison, follow US-151 S/US-18 W/Verona Rd for 37 miles. Merge onto US-18 W/Dodgeville Expressway via the ramp to Dodgeville/Prairie Du Chien. After the traffic circle, follow US-18 W for 11 miles. Turn right onto WI-80 N/N, Division Street and go about 3 miles.

Then turn right onto County Highway BH and travel for another 3 miles and turn right into the Blackhawk Lake Area.

♪ Blackhawk Lake sounds like "Surf City" by Jan & Dean to us.

http://goo.gl/maps/xW8IN

2. Castle Rock Flowage

The wooded shores of Castle Rock Lake, Wisconsin's fourth largest, are studded with numerous public launches. Over 25,000 acres of the shoreline remain in its natural beauty. The 60 miles of shoreline retain an undeveloped feel even though it is a very popular lake. The lake itself is over 16,000 acres and generally ranges from 8 to 30 feet in depth. Get a good day on the water behind you and stick around for some serious sunsets.

Head over to Buckhorn Barrens State Natural Area near Necedah for the lake's SUP sweet spot. The peninsula is a 4,500-acre water lover's paradise. You can launch from one of the suggested sites below or head over to the 300-foot sandy beach. When the wind is up, stick close to shore to avoid the chop. And if you're feeling natural, you can paddle the 10-stop Interpretive Canoe Trail. The trail can take 60–90 minutes and gives you a view of the open flowage at one spot. Weed growth may make the trail hard to navigate in the late summer.

Buckhorn Barrens also offers "cart-in" wilderness camping with many sites right on the water. Call (608) 565-2789 for more information or to reserve.

If you're thirsty, pop in at the Dirty Turtle in New Lisbon. They are known for their Bloody Marys and have a fun, lakeside atmosphere.

There are three launches to consider at Castle Rock.

Strongs Prairie Launch

The Strongs Prairie Launch is located at the north end of the flowage and is an hour north of Baraboo. Head out on 12 W for 6 miles until it intersects with I-90/I-94 W. Merge onto 90/94 W and drive 13 miles to Exit 79 for County Road HH. Turn right onto County Road HH, and after driving 6 miles, turn right on WI-82 E/WI-82 Trunk E and then take your first left onto County Road Z. After following Z for 15 miles, take a left onto Czech Avenue. A mile later follow the jog by turning right onto 20th Avenue and then left again onto Czech Avenue. Czech curves to the right and becomes 20th Court, which will lead to the launch.

Buckhorn Barrens State Natural Area

Canoe Launch A is an hour north of Baraboo. Head out on 12 W for 6 miles until it intersects with I-90/I-94 W. Merge onto 90/94 W and drive for 22 miles to Exit 69 for WI-82 toward Mauston and Necedah. Turn left onto WI-82 Trunk W. Then turn right onto WI-58 N after 1 mile. Continue on WI-58 for 9 miles and follow the road to the right as it becomes County Road G. Turn right onto Buckhorn Park Avenue after 4 miles on G. Follow Buckhorn Park Avenue for 1.7 miles and take a right on 36th Street and your destination will be on the left.

Canoe Launch B is an hour north of Baraboo. Head out

on 12 W for 6 miles until it intersects with I-90/I-94 W. Merge onto 90/94 W and drive for 22 miles to Exit 69 for WI-82 toward Mauston and Necedah. Turn left onto WI-82 Trunk W. Then turn right onto WI-58 N after 1 mile. Continue on WI-58 for 9 miles and follow the road to the right as it becomes County Road G. Turn right onto Buckhorn Park Avenue after 4 miles on G. Follow Buckhorn Park Avenue for 1.7 miles and take a left on 36th Street.

♪ The Castle Rock Flowage sounds like "The Lonely Surfer" by Jack Nitzsche to us.

http://goo.gl/maps/2jW1g

3. Delavan Lake

Delavan Lake is located in southern Wisconsin, about half an hour north by northeast of Beloit. With an average depth of 20 feet, this body of water offers a slightly quieter experience than its neighbor, Geneva Lake.

Delavan Lake is heavily developed and mostly private, but put in at the launch listed below and go find some quiet coves. The lake is creek and spring fed and recent water cleanup efforts have paid off for area groups, making Delavan a fine day trip, but try to hit it early in the day and early in the season, as it does crowd up.

There are a couple of launches on Delavan Lake, as it is such a popular lake. This set of directions will lead you to a quieter put-in than the main, paved boat launch. Once you are on I-43 N, go for about 20 miles and take Exit 21 to get on WI-50/E Geneva Street. Head east for 0.5 mile and then turn right onto N. Shore Road. The carry-in launch will be on your left.

♪ Delavan sounds like "Walk-Don't Run '64" by The Ventures to us.

http://goo.gl/maps/RiNff

4. Devil's Lake

Devil's Lake is the quintessential central Wisconsin lake. Called "Yellowstone of the Midwest" by some, this jewel is Wisconsin's most popular park. It receives over 1.5 million visitors per year. The 360-acre lake is surrounded by beautiful quartzite cliffs that rise up to over 500 feet. There are beaches at both ends of the lake, but only the north side is pet-friendly. No gasoline-powered motors are allowed on this lake, so get your Zen on as you glide through nature on your SUP. If you get hungry, there are concessions at both ends of the lake during the summer. After registering your vehicle, head to the South Shore for the best SUPing in the park.

Although no longer a cause for concern, Swimmer's Itch has been an issue at Devil's Lake in the past. As a precaution against the little fluke, wear waterproof suntan lotion and shower or towel off as soon as you exit the water. Reports of the rash have all but disappeared over the past few years.

There is plenty of good camping at Devil's Lake. Sites generally cost between $12 and $17. Call (608) 356-8301 for more information.

Devil's Lake State Park is only about 50 minutes north of Madison. Find your way over to US-12 and head west for 32 miles and then turn right onto WI-159. Head east for 1.5 miles and then turn right onto WI-123 Trunk S. The park entrance will be on the left.

♪ Devil's Lake sounds like "Surfin' U.S.A." by The Beach Boys to us.

http://goo.gl/maps/K6zEo

5. Geneva Lake

See SUPers and be seen paddling at this popular summer spot that lies about an hour southwest of Milwaukee. Geneva Lake is Wisconsin's second deepest lake at 135 feet. It is developed and a popular summer destination—as it should be! The water is inviting, it is spring-fed and has a sandy bottom. It is a good place to try out SUPing since there are rentals down by the main beach.

If you would like some lessons or to rent a board, check out Clear Water Outdoor at *www.clearwateroutdoor.com* and Fontana Paddle Company at *www.fontanapaddleco.com,* or Gordy's Marine at *www.gordysboats.com/marina/paddle-boarding*.

And if you are around in July, be sure to check out the Geneva Lake segment of the annual Midwest SUP Championship and Festival. For more information, check out *www. midwestsup.com*.

Leaving from Milwaukee, head out on I-94 W for abut 6 minutes and take the left exit, number 305A, for I-894/US-45 for Chicago. Follow US-45 south and then continue onto I-43 S for about 30 miles. Take Exit 27A for US-12 E toward Lake Geneva. Keep left at the fork and continue on for about 7 miles. Then take Exit 330A for WI-50 W/WI-120 S toward Lake Geneva. Turn right onto WI-120 S and go 1.5 miles and then turn left at Broad Street. Continue onto Wrigley Drive and your put-in will be on the right.

If the Geneva Lake put-in is cramping your style, find S. Lake Shore Drive and continue on around the lake to Bigfoot Beach State Park. The beach is across the street from the parking lot, but is often less crowded.

 ♪ Geneva sounds like "Surfer Girl" by The Beach Boys to us.

http://goo.gl/maps/HjBMf

6. Mirror Lake

Just three miles from the Dells, Mirror Lake offers paddlers of all stripes the natural beauty of a lake surrounded by 50-foot

tall sandstone bluffs. Over half of the narrow, clear lake is surrounded by the magnificent cliffs. The narrow lake is only 130 acres and is usually only about 10 feet deep. One of its main draws is that it is largely protected from the wind, giving the pine-tree shored surface its mirror-like glassiness. Even if popularity were to become an issue, there are no wakes allowed from any boat on Mirror Lake, so you are free to glide in aquatic peace here.

If you are planning to camp at Mirror Lake State Park, the daily fees are between $15 and $17. All the sweet spots for camping are non-reservable, so show up early and make some

friends with compadres shipping out. Call (608) 254-2333 for more information.

If you're feeling upscale this weekend, there is a Frank Lloyd Wright–designed cottage, called the Seth Peterson Cottage, for rent (to the public!) as well. Peterson convinced the ninety-year-old Wright to design the cottage for him in 1958, then he committed suicide before Wright was able to finish it for him. You can drool over the state-owned cottage here: *www.sethpeterson.org/*.

Mirror Lake State Park is ten miles north of Baraboo, Wisconsin. Head north on US-12 W for 5 miles and take Exit 212. Take the third exit from the traffic circle onto County Road BD. At the next traffic circle, take the first exit onto Fern Dell Road. Enter Mirror Lake State Park and follow signs to the launch.

♪ Mirror Lake sounds like "Lonely Sea" by The Beach Boys to our ears.

http://goo.gl/maps/wD4NE

7. The Yahara Chain

The Yahara chain of lakes easily sees the most SUP action in the state. Not only is there a good community built around the sport, excellent retail and instructional support, as well as the fun and forward-thinking city of Madison surrounding it, the lakes also have a group of water enthusiasts dedicated to their improvement. The descriptions and put-ins listed here are reprinted from the Yahara Waterways Trail Guide with gracious permission from its authors (see Appendix). The complete resource is a comprehensive and concise guide that we encourage people to download, peruse, and use.

To download or purchase hard copies, please visit: *www.danewaters.com/articles/guideDownload.aspx*

The Yahara watershed, or land area that drains into the Yahara River and lakes, covers 359 square miles, more than a fourth of Dane County. Much of the watershed is farmed; however, the watershed also contains most of the urban land of the Madison metropolitan area. In addition, the Yahara watershed includes some of the largest wetlands that are left in Dane County. The lakes' watershed includes all or parts of five cities, seven villages, sixteen towns, and is home to about 350,000 people.

Glaciers primarily shaped this area. About 15,000 years ago the glacier ice reached its maximum, with the Madison area covered by about 1,000 feet of ice. About 12,000 years ago, glacial Lake Yahara connected all the present lakes, standing about 12 feet higher than present Lake Mendota, and encompassed about twice the current water area. Moving glacial ice also widened the valleys, created hills in the shape of elongated teardrops (called drumlins), and created poorly drained areas where wetlands formed. Sometimes called "the Yahara River Valley," the area represents the far western edge of the last glacier advancement.

The ice also left glacial deposits of silt, sand, gravel, and rock up to 350 feet deep. These deposits dammed up the existing, larger pre-glacial valleys, and formed the Yahara chain of lakes. The region is typically flat with gently undulating hills, a result of the glaciers flattening hills and filling former valleys. The gentle relief resulted in slower-moving streams and rivers than those found in the southwestern Driftless Area of southwest Wisconsin that was not covered by glacial ice. The watershed area has rich, young (less than 15,000 years old) soils.

Between 1833 and 1835, federal surveyors mapped out southern Wisconsin. The Madison area was mapped from south to north in December of 1834. The lakes were then named First Lake (Kegonsa), Second Lake (Waubesa), Third Lake (Monona), and Fourth Lake (Mendota). It was known by the Native Americans as the Four Lake area, or "Taychopera" in the Ho-Chunk language.

In 1855, then-Governor Leonard J. Farwell was in the midst of leading Madison to unprecedented economic prosperity by establishing businesses and systematic land development promotion. As part of this promotion he decided that more romantic names were needed for the lakes. Frank Hudson, a surveyor and student of tribal lore, suggested a series of three syllable, euphonious names in Chippewa or Ottawa—Mendota, which he said meant "great," and Monona or "beautiful." Lyman Draper, the secretary of the State Historical Society, additionally suggested to Farwell the names Waubesa or "swan" (supposedly a settler killed an unusually large swan in that area); Kegonsa or "fish" Lake, as it was known for its good fishing; and Yahara for the Catfish River's name. That same year the state legislature approved the names.

As you use this water trail guide, you may notice blue reflective signs with white letters and numbers affixed to many piers. These signs, part of Dane County's voluntary Lake Property Numbering System, can help you in an emergency. Each lakeshore property on Lakes Mendota, Monona, Waubesa, and Kegonsa has been assigned a unique "lake address." The Mendota addresses begin with the letter "A"; Monona with "B"; Waubesa "C"; and Kegonsa "D." These numbers have been cross-referenced in the 911-computer system with the property street address.

♪ In its entirety, the Yahara Chain sounds like "Pressure-Drop" by Toot and the Maytals to us.

Lake Kegonsa

Lake Kegonsa is the southernmost and often the windiest of the Yahara River lakes, and is surrounded primarily by agricultural land. Its watershed covers 54 square miles. Lake Kegonsa is a highly eutrophic, moderately shallow drainage lake, formed when glacial deposits dammed the Yahara River. Much of the shore is covered by homes, with only 1.5 miles of shoreline in public ownership.

Fish Camp County Park was a place for carp seining for many years. The state stocked the lake with carp from 1881–1897, and by the 1930s about three quarters to one million pounds of carp per year were removed and sold for food from each of the lower three Yahara Lakes. Lake Waubesa, in particular, had an

abundance. The carp were placed in large water tanks on box-cars and sent to Chicago, New York, and southern states where they were sold as a delicacy. Small fish were canned at Nine Springs for animal feed, plowed under for fertilizer, and sold live to mink ranchers. The State ran these operations until 1976, when it transferred the business to the private sector. More recently, commercial fishermen used the area in early spring and late fall for unloading carp caught in gill nets. Now the park offers a canoe launch, public restrooms, accessible piers, walk-in fishing, and a fish cleaning area. The original 1937 storehouses for nets and boats have been restored.

 From I-39 N, take Exit 156 for US-51 N. Continue on it through Stoughton for about 12.5 miles and turn right onto County Highway AB. After 1.5 miles turn right onto Fish Camp Road and the park will be on the left. *http://goo.gl/maps/WGO3k*

Lake Kegonsa State Park opened to the public in 1967. The 342-acre property is a mix of woodland, restored prairie, wetlands, and lakeshore frontage. Because of the variety of eco-systems, it is common to see deer, fox, otter, raccoons, herons, ducks, geese, turtles, snakes, reptiles, and songbirds. The park has a number of Native American mounds along a self-guided trail located in a mature oak forest. Numerous historical, archaeological, and natural resource features are found here, as well as a boat launch, beach, hiking trails, and restrooms.

Coming from Madison, take Highway 12/18 E past Interstate 90. Turn right on Highway AB. At the T-intersection turn left. Then turn right on Door Creek Road. The park is at the end of Door Creek Road on the right.

♪ Lake Kegonsa sounds like "Telstar" by the Challengers to us.

http://goo.gl/maps/NHjH5

Lake Mendota

Lake Mendota is the largest of the Yahara Chain—three times larger than Lake Monona. Its watershed covers 217 square miles. The largest and northernmost of the four Yahara chain of lakes, Mendota strongly influences water quality downstream in Lakes Monona, Waubesa, and Kegonsa.

For SUPing we suggest the following put-ins:

James Madison Park: The park was formerly the site of the Conklin Ice House, which operated from 1854 until 1936. The ice house was half a block long and the building had sawdust-filled walls two-feet thick in order to store ice all summer. Today a concession operates from the park shelter.

From the Beltline, exit at US-151 N/John Nolen Drive. Stay with 151 and after about 2 miles, take a left onto E. Washington Avenue and then the first right onto N. Franklin Street.

http://goo.gl/maps/jScms

Gov Nelson State Park is on the northwest side of Lake Mendota. From downtown Madison, head west on University Avenue and turn right onto Allen Avenue. After a couple of miles turn right again onto Century Avenue, which will become County Highway M. Continue on M until you meet Oncken Road. Take a right and you'll be in the water before you know it.

 From Middleton, hop onto Century Avenue for 1.5 miles, continue ahead onto County Highway M and then turn right at Onken Road.

http://goo.gl/maps/Xg6jT

Mendota County Park is on the west side of Lake Mendota. It is an easy 15 minutes from downtown. From the Beltline Highway/ 12/14 W, exit left at 251B for Parmenter Street. Turn

 right onto Donna Drive and then right again onto Century Avenue. Turn right onto County Park Road and violà—surfs up!

http://goo.gl/maps/gA7v0

Governors Island, formerly part of Governor Leonard J. Farwell's property, was an island until the 1860s when it was connected to the north shore of Lake Mendota by a narrow causeway. This 60-acre "island" is heavily used by dog walkers and birders. Nearby are fishing and scuba diving "hot spots." Shallow water near the site is a great spot to observe migrating waterfowl and for spring bird watching.

From Interstate 39 N/90 W, take Exit 136B for WI-30 W toward Madison. Take the WI-113 N/Packers Avenue ramp and then a slight left onto Northpoint Drive. Take a left on Troy

 Drive and another left onto Main Drive and then another left onto Cinder Lane. Continue onto Governors Island Parkway.

http://goo.gl/maps/aW2NC

Be sure to check out the biggest SUP festival around. The Midwest Stand Up Paddle Festival is located at Bishops Bay Country Club in Middleton. The club and its pier are privately owned. The clubhouse was once the home of the bishop of the Roman Catholic Diocese of Madison. Call Gary Stone at (877) 473-1199 for more information.

♪ Lake Mendota sounds like "Surf Wax America" by Weezer to us.

Lake Monona

Lake Monona's watershed covers just over 40 square miles. The lake has a diverse fishery of perch, panfish, largemouth bass, northern pike, walleye, and muskie. It is a eutrophic (nutrient rich) drainage lake subject to urban runoff, nutrient loading, and intense boating pressure.

Brittingham Park: Built in 1910 and designed by John Nolen, it is the oldest surviving Madison park structure and is a National Historic Landmark. The Camp Randall Rowing Club and the city of Madison recently renovated the boathouse in exchange for a twenty-five-year lease of space for the club.

From John Nolen Drive, take a left onto N. Shore Drive and left onto W. Brittingham Place.

http://goo.gl/maps/7tyhx

Olin Park: In 1854, Olin Park was a water cure resort and sanitarium with a four-story hospital. The hospital failed after four years, and in 1866 was refurbished into a sixty-room, first-class hotel called the Lakeside House. As the first resort in the area, the hotel operated until 1877, when it was destroyed by fire and never rebuilt. The Olin Pavilion, now a park shelter rebuilt in 1995, was a historic hall used for dancing and other social events. A boat launch site is located at the park.

Olin Park and Turville Point are just east of John Nolen Drive near its intersection with E. Olin Avenue.

♪ Lake Monona sounds like "Apache" by The Shadows to us.

http://goo.gl/maps/mHcCq

Lake Waubesa

The Lake Waubesa watershed covers 44 square miles and the lake has nearly 1,000 acres of wetlands surrounding it. An archeological survey by W.G. McLachlan in 1914 found 188 Native American mounds in 42 separate groups surrounding Lake Waubesa. Perhaps no other lake region in Wisconsin can furnish greater evidence of the activity of the mound-building Native Americans. Public lands dominate the views from the lake, offering wooded shores and restored upland environments of native grasses. Very few piers encroach on the shoreline, while native submergent vegetation graces the lake bottom.

Babcock County Park is located at the outlet of Lake Waubesa into the Yahara River. The park is named after Stephen Babcock, a University of Wisconsin scientist who invented an inexpensive way of determining the butterfat content in milk. The park provides accessible piers, restrooms, a fish-cleaning area, vending, and camping. The Babcock Park lock and dam was built in 1938. Dane County operates the 10-foot-high dam that controls the water levels for Lakes Monona and Waubesa. By adjusting water levels, the county helps create favorable spawning conditions for game fish in Lakes Monona and Waubesa and the Yahara River.

The park is just to the west of Highway 51 in McFarland.

http://goo.gl/maps/0T0Aw

Goodland County Park, one of Dane County's oldest parks, was named after Governor Walter Goodland, who took office in 1943 at the age of eighty. He had been a teacher, lawyer, and newspaper publisher before serving as a Wisconsin senator and lieutenant governor. The park contains an effigy mound, three linear mounds, and an oval mound. It offers a beach, boat landing, restrooms, and vending.

From Highway 14 E, exit at County Road MM, which is south of Madison, and turn left at McCoy Road. Turn right again onto County Road MM. Turn left onto Goodland Park Road.

http://goo.gl/maps/7u03Q

Jaeger Canoe Launch is a Wisconsin DNR property named after Conrad and Ruth Jaeger who were long active in environmental and cultural preservation. Visitors can take the path on the northwest side of the property to Indian Mound Park where the Lewis Group of mounds is located. These consist of multiple conical and linear mounds, plus a 74-foot bear mound and an unusual hook-shaped mound. Some of these are burial mounds. The launch is below the dam at Waubesa and flows slowly down to the Fish Camp Launch at the launch of Lake Kegonsa.

Heading south on Highway 51 in McFarland, take a left onto Exchange Street and the next left onto Jaeger Road.

♪ Lake Waubesa sounds like "Rumble" by Link Wray to us.

http://goo.gl/maps/e6G9D

Lake Wingra

Lake Wingra is quite possibly the most popular spot for SUP in the Madison area. Lake Wingra is a small, shallow 345-acre lake, located in the near west side of Madison, with the University Arboretum along its southern edge. Its watershed covers 5.4 square miles. It is the only one of the Yahara Chain to keep its Ho-Chunk name.

Wingra Park has a boat launch and a concession that provides canoe, kayak, and paddleboat rentals. The Knickerbocker Ice House was once located here, and provided lake ice for refrigeration until the early 1900s. The park is home to a multitude of SUP events, demos, and classes throughout the entire season. This is one spot you've got to check out.

From W. Beltline Highway, take Exit 257 for Whitney Way and take a right on Whitney. Turn right at Odana Road. After 2 miles, take a left onto Monroe Street and after another mile, turn right onto Terry Place.

http://goo.gl/maps/QbVxc

For more information call:

Wingra Boats at: (608) 233-5332 or check them out at *www.wingraboats.com.*

Paddle Board Specialists at: (877) 473-1199 or check them out at *www.paddleboardspecialists.com.*

Rutabaga Paddlesports at: (608) 223-9300 or visit them online at *www.rutabaga.com.*

♪ Lake Wingra sounds like "Bombora" by the Atlantics to us.

SW River Sessions

8. Grant River: Short Cut Road to Black Jack Road

Difficulty: **Mellowww**

Distance: 9 miles

The Grant River runs through the geologically unique Driftless Area. The Driftless Area is a section of the upper Midwest that never had glaciers present on it. Since the soils and bedrock were never compressed in the same fashion that other areas of

Wisconsin were, there is a good deal of unique plant and animal life. Along the riverway you will see some pretty cool limestone outcroppings.

This highly mellow section of river is popular for tubing during the summer. So unless you want to share the river with too many large groups, hit this river early or late in the season. It rarely gets above waist deep, but does occasionally get past 6 feet.

Most of the land along the banks of the Grant is privately owned, so no camping riverside here.

The put-in is at **Short Cut Road**. Houses quickly disappear into the background as forest and hills give way to cornfields as the day progresses. Watch out for any stray herds of cows!

Put-In—Short Cut Road: From Lancaster take Hwy 81/35 N. After crossing the Grant River Bridge, Hwy 81 and 35 split, so you'll want to keep left to stay on 81. Just after the split, look for Short Cut Road to the (sharp) left. A little ways down the road, the river swings around to parallel the road. The put-in will be down a grassy bank on your left.

Take Out: Use the bridge access that is near **County HWY U**, just off of Blackjack Road. Continue on 81 W from the put-in, and turn left on Highway V S.

♪ The Grant sounds like "Mr. Rebel" by Eddie & The Showmen to us.

http://goo.gl/maps/Q3gsN

9. Kickapoo River: Wildcat Mountain State Park
Difficulty: **Easy Float**
Distance: 5 miles

Taking its name from the Algonquin word that means "man who goes here, then there," this gentle and winding river will have your head spinning after it takes you on a ride through Wildcat Mountain State Park. The incredible, scenic river has plenty of strainers, so be vigilant as you pass through.

Put-in: From Ontario, Highway 131 crosses the river multiple times. There are launches at tons of the bridges crossing the water. We recommend putting in at Bridge 5 and taking out just past Bridge 10, but scope them out and follow your feel.

The Kickapoo River is known for its quickly changing water levels. The river will rise quickly during and after heavy rain, and flooding is common. During high water, passing under tree branches and some bridges may become difficult. Check the weather and flow reports before you plan your trip. For more information visit: *http://waterdata.usgs.gov/nwis/uv?05407470*

Wildcat Mountain State park is an hour east of La Crosse. Take State Highway 33 E for 30 miles. Take a right onto State Highway 33 E Trunk E/South Street and follow it for 13 miles. The park will be on the right.

Camping at Wildcat Mountain State Park is almost worth the trip by itself, considering that it offers excellent hiking. The park sits atop a 400-foot ridge overlooking the Kickapoo valley and boasts several stunning overlooks. There is camping available on the river, but only at a few places. For more information call the State Park office at (608) 337-4775.

 ♪ The Kickapoo sounds like "King Of The Surf Guitar" by Dick Dale & the Del-Tones to us.

http://goo.gl/maps/68sW9

10. Lower Wisconsin: Three Sections

Difficulty: The surfing here is **Easier** than staying out of the sun!

The Lower Wisconsin is the longest undammed section of river in the state. At a whopping 92 miles of navigable water, you're sure to find your perfect stretch. It stands opposite many of the other rivers we recommend in that it is a "big river." In 1989, then-Governor Thompson signed this scenic riverway into law. It is a special place that encompasses roughly 79,000 acres. A nine-member state board actually exists to protect the aesthetic integrity of the gorgeous river and scenery. While there are many cool islands, the real treats are the hundreds of long sandbars that lend themselves to frequent breaks and excellent camping (if you happen to have a buddy with a canoe). Additionally, the sandbars are great spots to enjoy the hundreds of species of birds that inhabit the banks.

In 1673, Father John Marquette said, "The Wisconsin River is very broad with a sandy bottom forming many shallows which render navigation difficult. It is full of vine-clad is-

lands. On the banks appear fertile lands diversified by woods, prairies and hills. We saw oak, walnut, basswood and another kind of tree armed with long thorns." It is truly amazing that 340 years later you can paddle a surfboard down the same river and think very nearly the same thoughts. It is a testament to the forward-looking conservationist dialogue that the citizens of Wisconsin have undertaken.

When choosing a section to run on the Lower Wisconsin you should consider how much solitude you're looking for. You can choose to take a few hours on the water or even a week! The farther you get from Prairie du Sac, the fewer and fewer people you will see. Two-thirds of the visitors to the Lower Wisconsin use the stretch from Prairie du Sac to Spring Green. This is a popular river during the summer, so if you plan to go in high season, consider hitting it during the weekdays. And remember, no glass!

♪ Sounds like "Surfers' Slide" by Richie Allen & The Pacific Surfers.

Lower Wisconsin I: Gotham to Muscoda
Difficulty: **Big 'n Easy**
Distance: 7.5 miles

This stretch of the river is less popular than its neighbors to the north and east, but it is no less outstanding of a paddle. Setting out from the high, sandy banks at the Buena Vista Landing in Gotham, you'll navigate tons of sandbars and big, wooly islands. On from the sandy banks of Gotham, you will see the land slide into a fine selection of the "3 B's"—barrens, bottomland, and bluffs. Marvelous.

Put in at the Buena Vista Landing to river-right and set off through sandy banks, beaches, and sandbars; 1.5 miles from the put-in you will pass under the storied Bogus Bluff. Tall tales of treasures have been told about this steep, tree-covered bluff to the north of the river.

Continue past sandbars and beautiful bluffs for another 3.5 miles and you will pass Orion Boat Landing river-right. You will know you're close when you see the cluster of homes on the shore.

Take-out is 2 miles past Orion at the Victoria Riverside Park landing. The landing is river-left on a rocky peninsula. You will also see a covered pavilion nearby.

Put-in: From Highway 60 in Gotham, turn south onto Fulton Street, then west onto Oak Street. Keep following the road until you reach Buena Vista.

http://goo.gl/maps/EnAau

Take-out: From Highway 80 in Muscoda, turn east on E River Road. Then turn north onto 4th Street. Keep following 4th until you see the landing.

http://goo.gl/maps/VOHFO

Lower Wisconsin 2: Mazomanie to Arena

Difficulty: Intermediate
Distance: 6.5 miles
Suggested CFM: 3,000–10,000. Link to current conditions:
  http://on.doi.gov/OGhacH

This section of the river is the second of three choice cuts that we explore. Wide, shallow, and pristine, this particular section is one of the most scenic and fun in the state. By the time you reach your take-out in Arena, this route will have you saying "Hana Hou!" (Hawaiian for One More Time!)

LW2 takes you on a 6.5-mile soul session winding past shifting sandbars, grassy banks, treed islands, and tall, bold limestone cliffs. You'll encounter fantastic views, tons of wildlife, and wonderful places to stop for a quiet break. In fact, since it is owned by the state, you are allowed to camp without a permit on any island or sandbar that you encounter.

The best time of the year to paddle this stretch is early summer. This section can get fairly crowded during the middle of summer, but there is always plenty of room for all.

As soon as you put in at Mazomanie, head across the river to get river-right. The best channel is far right until you wind past the large cliffs of Ferry Bluff, or about 2–3 miles in. The Mazomanie "nude" Beach to your left will be a hard feature to miss. Once you pass Ferry Bluff, paddle back to the center and then gradually let the main channel take you to the left for the remainder of the journey.

After you are on the water, you will not see houses river-left until the Arena take-out. When the water is low, you can either hand-carry your stick over a sandbar to the launch or go down-river from the landing and paddle back up the dredged channel that hugs the shore.

Bring a hat! The river is wide enough that there is rarely any shade. During late summer it is a good idea to try to watch for "V" shapes in the water and try to navigate toward the bottom of the "V." This will help ensure that you don't bottom out and chew up your fins.

Put-in: Mazomanie Canoe Landing. Go north from the town of Mazomanie on Highway Y. The cement ramp and pier are next to the road where it runs parallel to the river. Parking is across the highway and there is a picnic area and restroom available.

Scan this code to get directions on your smartphone: *http://goo.gl/maps/gRHoM*

Take Out: Arena Boat Launch. Heading east from Arena on Highway 14, turn north on Village Edge Road. After the road veers to the west, turn north onto River Road. This road will dead end at the landing. There are shaded parking spots there.

Scan this code to get directions on your smartphone: *http://goo.gl/maps/Qz01z*

Lower Wisconsin 3: Millville Boat Landing to Bridgeport Boat Landing
Difficulty: **Niiiiiiccce**
Distance: 5.3 miles

The area surrounding the Wisconsin River as it nears its final resting place at the mouth of the Mississippi is a place of peace and grand beauty. Some say that this is the prettiest stretch of the river, but who could choose? Get to Millville and "Drop-in, Turn-on, and Bliss-Out." Oh, and don't miss the Bridgeport Landing, it's the last one before the confluence of the Big Muddy.

Put-in is surrounded by a steep ridge at the Millville Boat Landing. After a short time on the water, you'll need to choose a channel around some large islands. Less than two miles in, a railroad grade will appear river-right for approximately 1 mile. After this, the river will glide past swampy bottomland and numerous islands.

You'll know you're close to the Bridgeport Boat Landing at Highway 18 when the river fills with a few long and wooded islands. The take-out is river-left, above the bridge.

After your day on this segment, do not miss out on Wyalusing State Park. The 2,600-acre park has views from the bluffs that will stop you in your tracks. And a bonus day if you plan to camp overnight is a marked canoe trail through the backwaters of the Mississippi River maintained by the park.

Put In: From Wyalusing State Park head east on County Road X for 1 mile and turn left (east) on County Road C. The put in will be at the corner of County Road C and Barker Hollow Road in approximately 10 miles. *http://goo.gl/maps/Ypg44*

Take Out: From the put-in, head back down County Road C and take a right (north) on WI 18/ WI 35 N. The take out is at the bridge.

http://goo.gl/maps/txYRO

Call the park at (608)996-2261 for more information.

♪ The Lower Wisconsin Sounds like "Catch A Wave" by The Beach Boys to us.

11. Mississippi River
Difficulty: **Dude, What?**

The Mississippi River is one of the world's major rivers by size, diversity, and biological productivity. It flows 2,350 miles from its source at Lake Itasca through the center of the United States and out into the Gulf of Mexico. Only the Missouri River, the Nile, the mighty Amazon, and the Yangtze outrank its length. The Big Muddy's watershed stretches all the way from the Rocky Mountains in the west to the Alleghenys in the east.

Just to get your head around how much water courses through the veins of this river, consider that at Lake Itasca it takes 10 minutes for the equivalent of one semi-trailer of water to flow out of the lake into the Mississippi. While down in New Orleans, the equivalent of 166 semi-trailers of water flow past Algiers Point every second.

Many would not consider the river for SUPing (or canoeing for that matter) due to its multitude of currents and heavy commercial traffic, but done the right way and in the right spots, paddling the Mississippi is a rewarding experience.

Avoid dangerous currents found close to, but especially immediately above and below, all dams and stay clear of barges and towboats. The large vessels cannot stop or maneuver easily. They can create dangerous currents even when they are tied up. And not all hazards show up on any chart, so be cautious of wing dams and other submerged structures outside of the main channel.

In 2011, adventurer David Cornwaithe completed the incredible task of SUPing the entire length of the Mississippi. Can you believe it? Check out his inspiring adventure on *www.youtube.com* or *www.davecornwaithe.com*.

We recommend that you rent or bring a pontoon boat and put in near some of the locks listed here and go explore the backwaters and sloughs outside of the main channel. Enjoy paddling on this national treasure and working river. In mid- to late summer many of the backwaters will be filled with astounding water lilies and yellow lotus flowers.

Mississippi Pool 9
Between Lock and Dam 8 and 9: Genoa to Lynxville
Distance: 10 miles one way

Lock and Dam No. 8 is located in a bluff-lined valley on the Upper Mississippi River. Lock and Dam No. 8 includes a lock, a dam with moveable gates, 3 miles of dike, and two overflow spillways. The Corps of Engineers originally completed the facility in April 1937. For more information call the Army Corps of Engineers at: (608) 689-2625

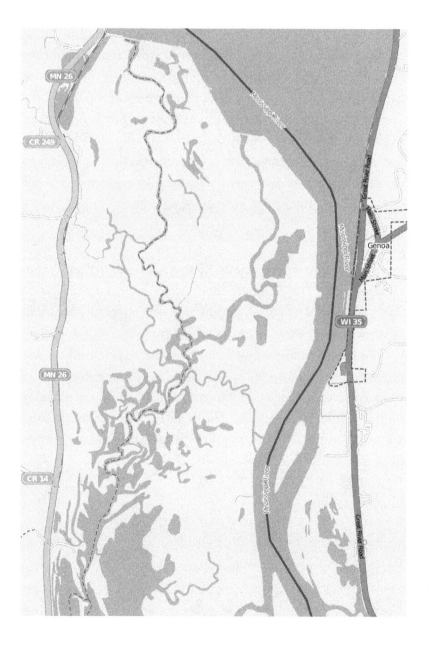

Take your SUP to the Minnesota side of the river at Genoa, Wisconsin, to *Reno Bottoms,* a 10-mile one-way trail that begins at the spillway for Lock and Dam 8 and goes to New Albin, Iowa, passing through backwaters that will twist and turn and meander until your head spins. Leaving the well-marked canoe trail can be the start of a very long day. If you get lost, pick up your board and follow the site of a bluff until you reach the shores.

For more information on this section contact Friends of Pool 9 at: *www.friendsofpool9.org/contact-us.html* or the Upper Mississippi Fish and Wildlife Refuge at: (507) 452-4232, or by visiting: *www.fws.gov/refuge/Upper_Mississippi_River/*.

Put-in at the **Reno Bottoms Canoe Trail** on the Minnesota side of Genoa, WI. Head south on WI-35 for13 miles and cross the river on WI 82 (right). Turn right on IA 26 N and continue as it becomes MN 26 N. Turn right onto County Road 249 after 17 miles. The put-in is a short way north of the city of Reno.

Mississippi Pool 6
Between Lock and Dam 5 and 6: Fountain City to Trempealeau

Old Man River takes a turn to the east from Fountain City to Trempealeau. You can actually see the sun rise and set over the path of the river on this section.

Trempealeau Mountain, now part of Perrot State Park, has long been sacred to the Winnebago and was used as a navigational aid for many of the founding years of the country. You can still see many interesting petroglyphs carved into the rocks overlooking what remains of the ancient mounds.

Relive some history on the **Voyageur Canoe Trail** at Perrot State Park. Voyageurs were French Canadian explorers that came through the area in the 1600s to expand the fur trade. Canoes were their primary means of transport. Explore

Trempealeau Bay as the voyageurs did on the 3.5-mile looped canoe trail. The trail is marked by blue and white directional signs and takes about 2–3 hours to complete. The river is strewn with islands between Winona and Fountain City.

From Trempealeau, head west on Park Road for 2 miles to the entrance of Perrot State Park.

Merrick State Park is a good choice for SUPing on this section. The 320-acre park is 3 miles north of Fountain City and provides easy access to the labyrinthine Whitman Bottoms. The park offers concessions, canoe rentals and firewood sales. It also offers campsites. Check out the Island Campground for sites with direct river access. For more information call the Park Headquarters at (608) 687-4936.

Drive north from Fountain City on WI-35 N for 3 miles and turn left (west) onto Park Road.

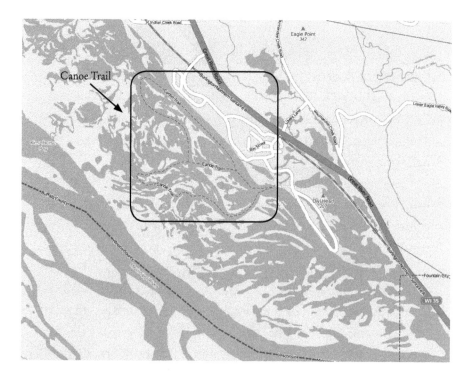

Mississippi Pool 5
Between Lock and Dam 4 and 5: Nelson to Alma

In Alma, at the boat landing near Highway 35 and the Dairy-land Power Plant, SUP out across the main channel (watch for boat and barge traffic) while angling north toward the islands. The 5.2-mile long **Alma to Finger Lakes Canoe Trail** enters through the islands and winds its way to Finger Lakes. There is one downed tree where you need to carefully navigate, but it is passable, or you can portage on land to the right.

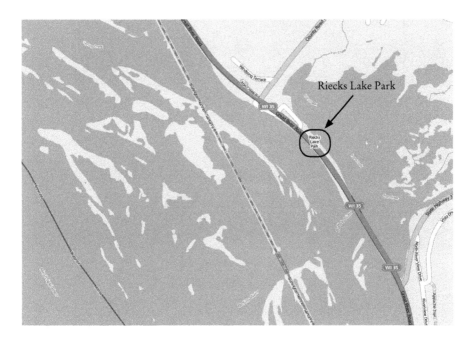

From Alma, take WI-35 north for 2.6 miles. **Rieck's Lake Park** is on the right side and **Brekow's Landing** is located to the left.

Paddle to the left out of Brekow's Landing until you reach the flowage from the Buffalo River out into Beef Slough. Beef Slough was a holding spot for logs in the nineteenth century.

Paddle to the right, going under the railroad bridge. At this point you are in Beef Slough; keep paddling to the right.

Follow the slough to the end and you will come to a sandy island on the Mississippi River. Pull your board up on the shore, relax, and have a look around. Leaving the island to the left you will return to the railroad bridge, pass under it river-left to return to Brekow's Landing, about 3 miles.

For more information on the many options you have for canoeing in Pool 5, contact Riverland Outfitters at (608) 385-4351.

Reiks Lake Park/ Brekow's Landing
http://goo.gl/maps/Rx7Kg

Merrick State Park/ Whitman Bottoms
http://goo.gl/maps/5kLhu

Lock and Dam 8/ Reno Bottoms
http://goo.gl/maps/D4gBQ

Trempealeau Mountain/ Perrot State Park
http://goo.gl/maps/LjVZG

♪ To our SUP ears, the Mississippi sounds like "Pipeline" by The Chantays.

Southeast Wisconsin

SE Flatwater Classics

I. Rock Lake

Rock Lake gives you the unique opportunity, possibly the only one in the entire world, of surfing pyramids. That's right! The southeastern Wisconsin lake holds within its depths ancient stone mounds that resemble pyramids. They are thought to be connected to the nearby Aztalan Mounds and the Woodlands culture that built the southern Illinois pyramid city of Cahokia.

The clear, figure 8–shaped, 1,300-acre lake lies in the town of Lake Mills, about 20 miles east of Madison, and is no deeper than 87 feet. There are two beaches to consider at Rock Lake for put-ins—the quaint Bartle's Beach and the popular Sandy Beach. This park offers two swimming beaches, picnicking, restrooms, boat rentals, boat launch facilities, and a seasonal restaurant.

If you are feeling thirsty after a long day paddleboarding atop the watery pyramids, stop over at the excellent Tyranena Brewing Company to sample some outstanding craft brews. They can be found at 1025 Owen Street in Lake Mills.

Rock Lake is accessible from I-94—a nice sandy beach lies just about 40 minutes east of Madison. Once you've been on I-94 E for about 20 miles, take the exit for WI-89 S/County Road G/N, Main Street. Turn right at the exit and then in about 2 miles, turn right onto Sandy Beach Road.

♪ Rock Lake sounds like "Atlantis" by The Shadows to our ears.

http://goo.gl/maps/ExEzk

SE River Sessions

2. Milwaukee River

The Milwaukee River is an SUP experience not to be missed. Rent a paddleboard from Laacke & Joys in downtown Milwaukee at 1433 N. Water Street and launch from their dock right at the store. Call (414) 271-7878 to reserve. Head up-river

to the Lakefront Brewery take-out near the Van Buren Street bridge on river-right (left if you're headed upstream), grab an excellent brew (only one now!) and head back down.

http://goo.gl/maps/0jIRV

3. Milwaukee Urban Water Trail

The Milwaukee Urban Water Trail is a canoe and kayak route through 25 miles of the urban portions of the Milwaukee, Menominee, and Kinnickinnic Rivers. Pass by all manner of attractions that include downtown Milwaukee, Milwaukee RiverWalk, Pabst Theater, Performing Arts Center, Milwaukee County Historical Society, Urban Ecology Center, Miller Park Stadium, and a number of boat marinas.

For a full listing of launch sites, download the map from: *www.mkeriverkeeper.org/content/milwaukee-urban-water-trail/*

♪ Milwaukee sounds like "Let's Go!" by The Routers to us.

SE Third Coast

4. Milwaukee

Milwaukee, the economic powerhouse in the southeast corner of the state, is home to over 500,000 people. If you include the entire metro area, it is well in the millions. There are numerous reasons to visit Milwaukee during the summer. The "beer city" has an incredible music festival, well-kept public beaches, and a good nightlife. Sounds like heaven for a stand up surfer, doesn't it? It is. You'll have your choice of Lake Michigan beach or ur-

Alex Marks

ban river here in Milwaukee. If you want to network with some like-minded SUP aficionados, hook up with Project Paddle at *www.projectpaddle.com/*.

Get down at **Bradford Beach.** Located at 2400 N. Lincoln Memorial Drive, this is where Milwaukee heads when it's hot. This lovingly rehabbed spot is now a matter of pride for the city. People head here for every manner of organized (and unorganized) sport and the party atmosphere is pumped up by the recently renovated Bradford Beach House. If you're feeling the vibe, you can even rent an SUP and a full-service beach cabana all at the same spot! Call (414) 502-7368 to reserve or get more information, or visit *www.bradfordbeachjam. com* and *www.bradfordbeachcabanas.com/Cabana_Co/ Welcome.html*.

http://goo.gl/maps/nP9iS

South Shore Park, at 2900 South Shore Drive, is a fairly small, narrow park along the shoreline south of downtown Milwaukee in the Bay View neighborhood. A stone breakwater protects the park, and yachts from the South Shore Yacht Club, which is located on the north end of the park, can be seen bobbing in the clear water throughout the summer. South Shore Park contains a cool pavilion located in the middle of the park. It was originally built as a bath-house in the 1930s. Check it out. Call the park office for more info at: (414) 482-4270.

http://goo.gl/maps/6GHlU

5. Racine

Wedged in between Milwaukee and Chicago is the 78,000-person city of Racine. Situated where the Root River meets Lake Michigan, this multifaceted city has one of the best beach experiences in Wisconsin just waiting for you and your paddleboard.

Make a beeline to **North Beach.** This beach has been designated a "Blue Water beach" since 2004 and the designation holds true today. North Beach features a beautiful beach and a host of other activities. It has a bath house, bicycle/walking path, nature center, shelter, and restrooms. The Oasis serves up tasty food and offers live music during summer weekends. *USA Today* actually calls it "one of the 51 Great American Beaches." Stop by and see why. From I-94, exit at Washington Avenue and take a right onto Washington. Stick with Washington for 5.5 miles and turn left onto S. Green Bay Road/WI-31 N. After a mile, take a right on Spring Street and follow it for

another 2 miles. Turn right onto Northwestern Avenue and continue ahead or slightly left onto State Street. Once you are on State, keep an eye out for Main Street and take a left onto it. Take a right onto St. Patrick Street and then continue to Hoffert Drive. North Beach will be on the right.

♪ Racine sounds like the "Peter Gunn Theme" by Henry Mancini (yeah, Henry Mancini).
http://goo.gl/maps/mEl4N

Northeast
Wisconsin

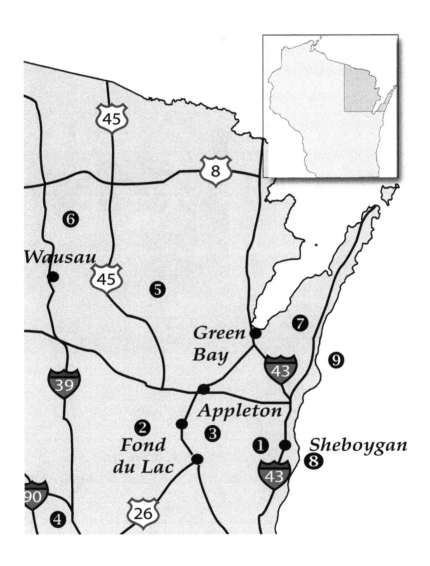

NE Flatwater Classics

1. Elkhart Lake

C.R.Y.S.T.A.L. C.L.E.A.R.
is the name of the game
at Elkhart Lake. Known
more for its vintage car
road races than water, this
little patch of awesome-
ness is 20 minutes west of
Sheboygan. Head over to
Fireman's Park for some
stand up paddleboarding
sun and fun. The lake has
a sandy bottom and is su-
per clean. You'll feel like
you are paddling south of

Florida, not north of Milwaukee! Hit your suntan lotion hard
though, because there isn't much shade cover at the sand and
grass beach.

For a $3 admission fee, you get access to well-maintained
beaches, bathrooms, and sand volleyball courts. The concession
does burgers and beers, or bring your own to grill. During the
summer you can check on the live music schedule as well.

Once you're in Sheboygan, look for WI-23 W/Kohler Memorial Drive. Continue on WI-23 W for just under 15 miles
and then turn right onto County Road P. Turn right again onto
County Road P/Kettle Moraine Scenic Drive and continue for
about 2.5 miles. Turn onto French Road and your launch will be
to the left.

♪ Elkhart Lake sounds like "Let's Go Trippin'" by Dick Dale & the Del-Tones to us.
http://goo.gl/maps/iH80q

2. Green Lake

Green Lake is Wisconsin's deepest inland lake. It is only about an hour northeast of Portage and about 30 minutes from where you leave the Interstate. The spring-fed lake averages about 100 feet in depth, but can delve as deeply as 237 feet! Once you put in, who knows, maybe you'll be skimming right over Nessie's head.

There are three decent choices for put-ins at Green Lake. They are Sunset Park, Dodge Park, and the Hattie Sherwood Campground. Sunset is wide open, so you'll see more boats there. While Dodge and Hattie both have good sand, we recommend Hattie Sherwood since it has decent bathrooms. Call (920) 294-6380 or visit *http://www.hattiesherwood.com* for more information. Tent sites are $28 a night and the daily boat launch fee is $5.

Hattie Sherwood Park is a good surf launch for Green Lake. There is also a campsite there if you are on an SUP safari.

In Portage, get on I-39 N/US-51 N for about 15 miles and sidle off at Exit 106 for WI-23. Head toward WI-82 W/Oxford for 0.5 mile and turn right onto WI-23 E. Stay on that for about ten minutes and take a right onto S. Lawson Drive. Stay on Lawson for a mile and then turn left onto White Oaks Street. White Oaks will veer to the right and become Bluff Street and you'll hit your destination head-on.

If you're feeling a little peckish after pushing that paddle, hit the Boat House Pub in Green Lake after your day out. They're known for their onion rings, and have nice outdoor seating and sweet views of the lake.

♪ Green Lake sounds like "Crusher" by The Atlantics to us.

http://goo.gl/maps/1yMds

3. Lake Winnebago

Huge Winnebago is over 30 miles long and 10 miles wide. It's the largest inland lake in the state and a sight to behold. It was formed when the glaciers began to melt, but a portion of them was blocked entering Lake Michigan by the land surrounding present-day Green Bay. The lake is generally about 15 feet deep and gets no deeper than 20 feet. Although it is quite large, it will eventually warm up during the season. For the best paddling, head out to either High Cliff State Park or Calumet County Park. The water can be murky, but both of these spots are worth a day trip.

High Cliff is situated on the northeast part of the lake and offers camping, hiking, great views of the lake, a marina, beach, and an observation tower. While you're there be sure to check out the effigy mounds left by the Native Americans.

The park's marina and general stores offer concessions from Memorial Day through Labor Day. Campsites are available for $12–$17 daily. Vehicle admission stickers are required to get into the park. Daily in-state rates are $7, while out-of-state tags will set you back $10.

Calumet County Park is a 200-acre park lying on the eastern shore of the lake. Along with lakefront camping and bathing facilities, the park features numerous panther-shaped effigy mounds and the part of the Niagara Escarpment cliff band. Daily camping fees are $18 to $20. Head on down to the launch and get going.

Calumet County Park, in Herbert, rests on the northeast side of Lake Winnebago and it's only 30 minutes from down-

town Fond du Lac. Hop on US-151 northbound for 20 miles. Continue driving onto WI-55 N for another 7 miles and turn left onto County Road EE.

http://goo.gl/maps/XvNiY

High Cliff State Park is on the northeast side of Lake Winnebago and it's only 40 minutes from downtown Fond du Lac. Get yourself onto US-151 northbound for 20 miles. Continue driving onto WI-55 N for another 11 miles and turn left onto WI-114 Trunk W/ WI-55 N. After a mile, turn left onto Clifton Road. Continue onto Spring Hill Drive, and then turn left onto State Park Road after a mile.

♪ Lake Winnebago sounds like "Honolulu Lulu" by Jan & Dean to us.

http://goo.gl/maps/s2Evt

4. Lake Wisconsin

With 52 miles of shoreline and views that won't quit, Lake Wisconsin is a must for SUP. Unbelievable views of the water and the rolling hills that flank the lake will surround you as you push your way past numerous sandbars in this impoundment of the Wisconsin River. Formed by the construction of a dam at

Prairie du Sac in 1915, this reservoir provides flood control for the lower Wisconsin river basin.

Hop the unique car ferry at Merrimac and begin your Lake Wisconsin surf soul session. A couple of good places to push a board are from the Happy Hollow Park or the Pine Bluff access that are both just a few minutes north of Lodi.

After a day out on the water, enjoy the sunset from the Lakeside Bar and Grill in Poynette. They've got good views of the lake and have a fun "lakeside" atmosphere to enjoy dinner and drinks.

The Happy Hollow Park launch is about 15 minutes north of Lodi. Peel out of town using WI-60 Trunk E/Portage Street and take a left onto Lindsay Road. Head straight as the road becomes County Road J and continue for 2.5 miles (do not turn right to follow County Road J). Take a right onto Smith Road and follow it for 1.5 miles. Take a left onto County Road CS and then take your second right onto County Road V. Turn Left into the park and follow signs to the launch. *http://goo.gl/maps/Q6e5z*

The Pine Bluff launch is only about 5 minutes north/northwest of Lodi. Head out of town on WI-113 N for 4 miles and turn right on County Road V. After 0.5 mile, continue onto Summerville Park Road and turn right onto Bay Drive.

 ♪ Lake Wisconsin sounds like "Moon Dawg" by The Gamblers to us. *http://goo.gl/maps/sDJNb*

5. Shawano Lake

"Shawano" is derived from the Menominee word for south. But whichever direction you take to get there, you'll be sure to enjoy this destination. The lake is a hard water drainage lake 40 miles northwest of Green Bay. The popular, if shallow, fishing

lake flows out into the Wolf River. It is generally only 9 feet deep and covers over 6,000 acres.

The best place to launch is from the Shawano County Park, which is located on the north shore of Shawano Lake on County Highway H. This 32-acre park has a wooded area with 90 campsites on approximately 18 acres with showers, camp store, restrooms, and a 300-foot sand beach and boat launch.

Campsites will set you back $20, and if you're willing to part with $40 you could find yourself snoozing in a tipi! Reserve one by calling (715) 524-4986.

Head out of town on WI-29 W for 1.5 miles, continue onto WI-29 W/Trunk W for another 14 miles and continue onto WI-47 N for another 6 miles. Take Exit 227 to merge onto WI-47 N/ WI-55 N and continue onto Airport Road/County Road HHH. County Road HHH curves to the right and becomes County Road H/N, Lake Drive. Look for County Park signs and follow them to the launch.

♪ Shawano sounds like "Perfidia" by The Ventures to us.

http://goo.gl/maps/Wir5c

NE River Sessions

6. Pine River: Oxbow County Highway N Landing to WEPCO Landing #5
Difficulty: **SWEET**
Distance: 3.5 miles

The mostly undeveloped Pine River will have you humming something akin to these surf tunes we're listing as soon as you push out on your paddleboard. It is a designated wild river. The red and white pine forests are only broken by stands of beautiful birch and awe-inspiring aspen.

The Oxbow trip is one of the best shuttles in Wisconsin. Just drop your SUP off at the County N Landing, drive down to the next bridge and hoof it back up to the boards and buddies.

Paddle it up and hop out at the next bridge you see. The take-out is opposite a steep, wooded bank.

Check out nearby Iron Mountain, Michigan, for food and accommodations after you've "ox-d the bow."

The Pine is usually navigable throughout spring, summer, and fall. The Pine Dam, which is located 2 miles above the Highway N Wayside Landing, feeds it. For more information about river conditions call (906) 779-2518

Put-in: Heading west on North County Road from Iron Mountain, Michigan, turn north/right on County Highway N. The put-in will be at the bridge over the river.

Take-out: WEPCO Landing #5. From the County N Bridge, head north for 4 miles and veer right to stay on County Highway NN. Turn right with County Highway NN, then take the first right onto US-141 S/US-2 E. Continue for 6 miles and take a right onto Lake Ellwood Road. After 2 miles, turn left onto Menominee River Road and then turn right onto Town Road DD.

♪ The Pine sounds like "The Inebriated Surfer" by The Tornadoes to us.

Put-in and Take-out: *http://goo.gl/maps/L2158*

NE Third Coast

7. Door County

Door County is the ever-popular vacation destination on the 71-mile Door Peninsula that juts out into Lake Michigan on Wisconsin's northeast side. The peninsula and county are named for the Door Strait, which was long known as treacherous waters

to the French and Native Americans. In fact, its original name meant "Death's Door" in French. The beginning of every summer brings a tourism-driven explosion in population. Because of this seasonal influx, you'll find every manner of amenity during your visit.

There are numerous beaches dotting the shoreline near almost every city. We'll list some highlights here, but stick close to the 300 miles of shoreline and you're bound to find a favorite spot.

Egg Harbor was once named "One of the Coolest Small Towns in America" by *Budget Traveler* magazine. Could it be the expansive sky and the bright blue water? Or maybe it's the new marina? Or possibly the live music? Stop in and decide for yourself. The best place to paddle there is Beach Park, located at 4736 Beach Road. It features a sandy beach, pavilion, playground area, and wonderful swimming. DC Adventures offers SUP rentals and instruction. Call (920) 746-9999 for more infor-

mation. To get there, take Highway 42 from Sturgeon Bay
to Highway G and then turn west at the first stop sign.

http://goo.gl/maps/NYt7a

Whitefish Dunes State Park is an 865-acre park that protects the large yet fragile dunescape near Sturgeon Bay. The park holds a beautiful, long beach set back in a cove. It will seem like you're surfing an exotic island. A word of caution: the concave bend of Whitefish Bay forms tough riptides. Predicting where these currents form is never entirely possible and lifeguards are never on duty. This is an easy paddle if it is a calm day, but can be a challenge if the wind picks up. To get there, take State Highway 57 northeast from Sturgeon Bay about 10 miles to Clarks Lake Road (County Highway WD). Turn right on Clarks Lake Road and go about 3.8 miles. Turn right onto the park entrance road to the greeting center and parking area. For more information call: (920) 823-2400.

http://goo.gl/maps/qpgQU

Cave Point County Park is often overlooked since it doesn't have a state or national designation, but that doesn't mean that it doesn't has something special in store. If you can pick a calm, wind-free morning, you'll be treated to a view of the Dolomite cliffs and caves that few visitors enjoy. Put in at Shauer Park, a little to the north of the park. The launch is difficult to see from a distance. The water is quite shallow and you may need to walk out for a short distance to avoid scrapping the bottom of your board. If the weather isn't cooperating, hit up the park's protected neighbor, Clark Lake.

From Sturgeon Bay, drive north on Highway 42/57 and curve left to stay on WI-57 for 6 miles. Turn right on County Road WD/Clark Lakes Road for another 3.5 miles and you will enter the park.

http://goo.gl/maps/qpgQU

Follow your internal SUP radar over to Nicolet Beach. Located in the 3,700-acre Peninsula State Park, you'll find another Wisconsin SUP hotspot. The concessions will gladly rent you a paddleboard. Call them at (920) 854-9220 for more information. Kayak Door County also offers Stand Up lessons here. Call (920) 818-0431 for more on them. Peninsula also offers camping for $15–$17 per night. All sites are within a 5-minute walk to the shoreline. It is an extremely popular camping destination in the

summer, but there are a few non-reservable sites if you don't choose to book ahead. If you have questions, call the office at (920) 868-3258.

http://goo.gl/maps/su9yD

Take the ferry from Northport Pier on Highway 42 to Washington Island and leave the hustle and bustle of lower Door County behind. The island is six miles from the mainland and, at 35 square miles, is the largest of the thirty islands in Door County. Rent a car and go over to the other end of the island and hit Schoolhouse Beach. You won't find any sand here, but the smooth stones, clear water, and general awesomeness more than make up for its absence. Passenger fare is $13 and autos are $26. For more information on seasonal schedules call (800) 223-2094 or visit *www.wisferry.com*. After a day swimming and SUPing, head over to the social hub of the island, Nelsen's Hall Bitters Pub, at 1201 Main Road to join the Bitters Club and grab a burger.

♪ Door County sounds like "Goldfinger" by The Blue Stingrays to us.

http://goo.gl/maps/xlDnr

8. Sheboygan

http://goo.gl/maps/uQTFp

Known to some as the "Malibu of the Midwest," Sheboygan has long been the proud standard bearer for surf and SUP in the Badger State. Sheboygan is a terrific 50,000-person town north of Milwaukee on Lake Michigan.

First stop is EOS Outdoor/Revolution Board Shop to rent a board, schedule a lesson, or get the lowdown about what's bangin'. Call (920) 208-7873 for more information or to reserve equipment. The shop is at 347 Kohler Memorial Dr.

Alex Marks

Alex Marks

Then cruise on down to Deland Park. It is centrally located and has a nice grassy slope before the expansive beach. The beach is adjacent to a very nice protected harbor, so during the summer there will be little wave action. Exit I-43 at WI-23 E. Follow WI-23 for 2 miles and turn left onto N. 14th Street. After a few blocks, turn right onto Michigan Avenue then after a mile, turn right onto Broughton Drive.

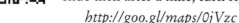

http://goo.gl/maps/0jVzc

Deland Park is also home to the world's largest fresh water surf competition, the Dairyland Surf Classic. You can really feel the community spirit of the organizers while you are there. Read how they describe it and you'll see what we mean: "Everyone is welcome to attend the Dairyland Surf Classic presented by PACIFICO. In the true meaning of the Aloha spirit, it's a gathering of community to celebrate freshwater surfing. It's a great place to meet new friends and check out the surf scene. You can watch the competition from the beach, or you can join the competition for a nominal registration fee. Either way, all are welcome to the annual Aloha Awards Banquet at Deland Park. It's a classic evening under the stars with pot-luck dinner, live music, and camaraderie. Open to the public, the only admission is bringing a dish to pass or something to grill!"

You can also check out the friendly SUP-N-Surf EOS series in late June. It is a leg of the Midwest Stand Up Paddleboard Championship Series. Visit *www.midwestsup.com* for more information.

Alex Marks

Two miles south of Sheboygan is the scenic Kohler Andrea State Park. Long known as a (secret shh!) surf spot in fall and winter, this park makes for good SUPing as well. Paddle down miles of golden, sandy beaches with the backdrop of protected dunes that are exactly as nature intended for the Lake Michigan shore. There isn't a boat launch, but hand carry is just fine. Conditions can be windy here. Vehicle admission fees apply. Traveling north from Milwaukee on I-43, take Exit 120 and go east on Highway V about two miles. Where Highway V turns left (north), continue straight onto Beach Park Lane, which is the park entrance road. Year-round camping is available for $12–$17 for a tent site or $34 to sit pretty in a tipi.

 ♪ Sheboygan sounds like *Malibu Babylon* by The Blue Stingrays to us.

http://goo.gl/maps/651FP

9. Two Rivers

http://goo.gl/maps/iiqAn

 Two Rivers is an 11,000-person town on the Lake Michigan shoreline that is about an hour and a half drive north from Milwaukee. Any city with a slogan like "Catch Our Friendly Waves" is worth any SUPer's visit! One cool claim to fame is their (hotly debated) stance that they

are the "Birthplace of the Ice Cream Sundae." We side with them of course, but don't ask anybody in Ithaca, New York. Neshotah State Park Beach is a 50-acre fun-filled, popular beach on Zlatnik Drive. The park is located off the intersection of Highway 42 and County Highway O.

♪ Two Rivers sounds like "Surfer Joe" by The Surfaris to us.

Northwest Wisconsin

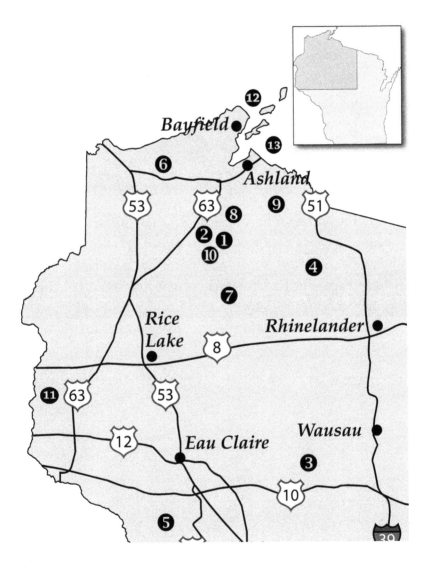

Bayfield

Ashland

Rice Lake

Rhinelander

Eau Claire

Wausau

NW Flatwater Classics

l. Lake Namekagon

Lake Namekagon is a 3,000-acre glacial lake within the borders of the massive Chequamegon National Forest and sits about 45 minutes south of Ashland. Packing up your board and heading to this lake will literally surround you with the Great Northwoods. Although this lake is a popular boating lake, paddleboarders will find a great day out exploring the many bays, inlets, and islands that the lake has to offer.

If you can make it out in the fall, there is a unique paddling opportunity at the Stand Up Paddleboard Color Tour and Race. See the beautiful fall colors at your own pace or join in the Island Hop race. If you're feeling feisty, join in the fun during the

afternoon races. If you would like more info, check out *www. lakewoodsresort.com/events/fall-winter-events/stroke-color.*

There are two launches to consider. One of them is from the town of Grand View and the other in the town of Namekagon.

Grand View: From Ashland, get on US-2 S for a couple of miles and continue through the traffic circle. Stay with US-2 for 6 miles and then turn left onto US-63 S. Stay on US-63 for 15 miles. Turn left onto County Highway D and go for 10 miles. Continue onto Missionary Point Drive. The Grand View launch will be on the left.

Town of Namekagon: From Ashland, get on US-2 S for a couple of miles and continue through the traffic circle. Stay with US-2 for 6 miles and then turn left onto US-63 S. Stay on US-63 for 15 miles. Turn left onto County Highway D and drive for 14 miles and the launch will be on your right.

 ♪ Namekagon Lake sounds like "Misirlou" by Dick Dale & the Del-Tones to us. *http://goo.gl/maps/PPqPf*

2. Lake Owen

Lake Owen is another Northwoods gem in Bayfield County. Its ultra-clear waters stretch over 9 miles and are over 95 feet deep in places. Most of the lake is part of Chequamegon National Forest, so soon after launch you'll feel like you're truly in the Great Outdoors—because you will be! In fact, Lake Owen was recently named Wisconsin's healthiest lake.

The Two Lakes Campground is 5 miles south of Drummond and sits between Lake Owen and Bass Lake. Many of the sites are right on the water, so bring a tent and launch in the morning! Fees are $18 for a site and $8 to use the launch or the beach if you're not camping. Call (715) 739-6334 for more information.

The Cable, Wisconsin, area is fast becoming an SUP hotspot. Head over to town for one of the largest selections of SUP paddling equipment, demos, lessons, and clinics by A.C.A.-certified instructors, trips and tours around.

One good SUP launch on Owen Lake is from the Twin Lakes Campground, which is about 45 minutes south of Ashland. From Ashland, get on US-2 S for a couple of miles and continue through the traffic circle. Stay with US-2 for 6 miles and then turn left onto US-63 S. Stay on US-63 for 21 miles. Turn left onto Fr 213/N, Lake Owen Drive and continue on it for 6 miles. Turn right into the Twin Lakes Campground and follow markers to the launch.

♪ Owen sounds like "Baja" by The Astronauts to us. *http://goo.gl/maps/tbp1c*

3. Lake Petenwell

At over 23,000 acres, this sandy and rocky man-made lake checks in at Wisconsin's second largest. Built in 1948 by the Wisconsin River Power Company by constructing a dam across the Wisconsin River, Lake Petenwell is a popular spot for water sport activities during the summer.

Your best bet to cut through some chop will be to head over to Petenwell County Park, the second largest county park in Wisconsin. This 160-acre, year-round park offers a designated swimming area, boat launch, playground equipment, and hiking trails.

At Petenwell, you can have it all. You can really feel like you've gotten away, yet have numerous dining and entertainment options once you're off the water. Check out the Lure Bar and Grill at Barnum Bay Marina for decent grub and a beachside Tiki Bar, or head into Necedah, Mauston, or New Lisbon for your pick of the restaurant litter.

Drive north from Portage on I-39/US-51 for 33 miles and take Exit 124 for WI-21 heading toward Coloma/Necedah. Take the left onto WI-21 and continue for 15 miles. Next, take a right onto WI-13 N/WI-13 Trunk N. After about 7 minutes turn left onto County Road C. Keep on going for another 8 minutes and take a right on County Road Z. Take your first left onto Bighorn Drive. In about a mile you will take a right onto 20th Avenue and then another right into the park.

 ♪ Lake Petenwell sounds like "Surfer's Stomp" by The Marketts to us.

http://goo.gl/maps/KxJJf

4. Turtle Flambeau Flowage

Want a trip to the boundary waters without a permit or passport? If an expansive wilderness experience is the scene you crave, look no further than the Turtle Flambeau Flowage. The sprawling wilderness complex includes over 19,000 acres of water, or 30 square miles, and is surrounded by 210 miles of winding wooded shoreline and 35,000 acres of public land.

Built in 1926 to provide power to a local paper mill, this region was officially designated a protected wilderness area in 1992. Its rugged natural beauty has largely been preserved. The flowage has numerous sand bars, rock bars, islands, floating driftwood, and other water features that can make motorized water sports hazardous, so pushing your way around on an SUP is an ideal way to spend a day (or more!) here.

Try putting in at Lake of the Falls County Park on the north end of the flowage on County Highway FF. It offers a boat launch and camping is available. Reserve by calling: (715) 561-2922. From Mercer, head north on WI-51 and turn left (west) on County Road FF. The park will be on your right in a couple of miles.

http://goo.gl/maps/Kv4gF

The Turtle Flambeau Flowage also offers remote campsites accessible by water only. They are available year-round on a first-come, first-served basis with no fee. Maps are available from the Mercer Ranger Station: (715) 476-2240.

Pontoon boats are also available to rent if you'd like to take gear overnight to some of the camping spots and to scope out the best SUP spots before getting in.

For info on pontoon rentals, visit one of the following:
Balsam Ridge Lodging & Pontoon Rentals
4335N. Kimmear Road
Mercer, WI 54547
(715) 476-0042

Donner's Bay Resort
2974 Hiawatha Road
Butternut, WI 54514
(715) 476-2555

Midway Pontoon Rental
89281 County Highway F
Butternut, WI 54514
(715) 769-3680

♪ Turtle Flambeau sounds like "Stoked" by The Beach Boys to us.

NW River Sessions

5. Black River: Melrose to North Bend
Difficulty: **Easy-Peazy**
Distance: 9 miles

John C. Elliot of the Friends of the Black River was kind enough to contribute the following:

> The Black River starts as a small stream flowing out of Black Lake in northern Taylor County. It flows for nearly 200 miles before emptying into the Mississippi River near La Crosse, Wisconsin. The Black River flows through land with sandy shallow soils and many wetlands. As the water filters through the wetlands, organic acids leach out of decaying wetland plants and other organic material causing the black coloration of the river. The stained water isn't harmful and actually limits the growth of noxious algae blooms or nuisance plants that would otherwise interfere with recreational activities.

I've had my share of water-related adventures over the years. Since I moved here from the flatlands of eastern Wisconsin about fourteen years ago, I have happily discovered the Black River in west-central Wisconsin offers both Class III whitewater as well as flatwater paddling. We also have three drop-dead gorgeous streams that are among the best in the state. It's so very nice to have choices between adrenaline rush versus quiet floats while meandering past cliffs and soaring eagles.

The Black River is called "flashy," as in flash floods. On the whitewater section below Lake Arbutus, the adventure should include a careful check of river data and some common sense planning. There are almost monthly releases at the dam. Information is available from the Hatfield Dam operators. For more information contact the Black River State Forest at (715) 284-4103.

My favorite contemplative paddle trip starts at the David Hanson Landing, which is situated in a tree-covered spot in the town of Irving. From Hanson's Landing, the trip can vary from one to several hours depending on the paddler's ambition. There are at least four outfitters in the area that offer canoes and kayaks as well as float tubes.

A person paddleboarding the quieter waters below the dam in Black River Falls can start from several put-ins. A great place to "hang ten" on the Black River is to put in at Melrose and take out at North Bend. This 9-mile trip will take you most of the day so don't forget to take some water and a snack. You'll find inviting sandbars seemingly around every corner of the trip, so make sure to stop frequently, chill, rinse, and repeat. This stretch is fairly isolated and wanders past beautiful, cliff-dotted, wooded shores.

Downstream from the put-in you'll see some low, scrubby islands after the bridge. Take your pick on which side of the island to attack.

When the river bends to the left, you'll see a long, tall, and steep sandy bank on the right. Farther downstream, as you encounter a tall river-right cliff band, pull off at the narrow break in the wall and check out the little canyon.

After passing the inlet of Davis Creek, you'll see an impressive band of cliffs on the right that reach out over the water. The cliffs hang onto the river for a long while, eventually curving right and then back left. After a time, with rock formations dotting the shores, the cliffs re-emerge and they continue straight until a right curve in the river-flow before straightening back out once again.

At the large island, keep right (as the sign advises) and take out just upstream of the Riverview Inn.

After you take out, duck into the Riverview Inn. They are a full-service supper club with good dining options and great views of the river. For more info visit: *www.riverviewinn.biz/*.

 Put-in: DNR Landing at Melrose, Wisconsin. From Melrose, head south on Highway 108 for 1.5 miles. Cross the river and turn left into the launch site.
http://goo.gl/maps/bJnHj

Take-out: North Bend, Wisconsin. Once you are in North Bend, take a right (southeast) onto N. Bend Drive. *http://goo.gl/maps/NQU9N*

Note: You probably shouldn't push off under 200 or above 3,000 CFS on the Black.

♪ The Black River sounds like "Surfin' Bird" by The Trashmen to us.

6. Bois Brule River: Stone Bridge to Winneboujou Landing
Difficulty: **Aggro**
Distance: 8 miles

While some conversationalists might take you up on the subject, there is a real case to be made that the Bois Brule River, from Stone Bridge on down to its terminus at the mouth of Lake Superior, is one of the finest river stretches anywhere in the Midwest—let alone Wisconsin. Offering SUPers of almost any skill level a run to remember, this beautiful, natural river lies within the massive 52,000-acre Brule River State Forest.

The Stone Bridge to Winneboujou leg is a very popular section. And if you take your board, you'll find out why. The landscape in this section of the Bois Brule will begin with boreal forest strewn with open marshes and slowly gives way to hills covered with aspen and maple forests. The banks of the river will then get even steeper before mellowing back out into open marshland, where it finds its home on the banks of Lake Superior.

While you're out, keep an eye peeled for osprey, eagles, and songbirds of every stripe.

There are rapids on this stretch so make sure that you are comfortable with your SUP before striking out on this journey. Check your map for points where the Class 1 and 2 rapids occur and pull off the river before attempting them for the first time.

Take the time to scope them out and check for any downed trees that may be in your way. It is highly recommended to never SUP on a river by yourself or to use a leash while on a river as the threat posed by submerged entrapments is too great.

At the well-developed Stone Bridge Landing, you will encounter 2.5 miles of chill, narrow river surrounded by dense forest.

The river will eventually widen to a pool with an island in its center. This is Rainbow Bend. After you pass the island, the Bois Brule will hang a right and after you pass the slough on river-left, you'll find lowland cedar forests replacing the grasslands.

After a right turn, the river will get narrower and you'll hit the Class 1 Mays Rips Rapids. You should begin to see some clear waters after these.

About 0.3 mile after Mays Rips, the river will fork around a number of islands. Sticking to the left you'll pass the Cedar Island Estate, which is a very popular fishing resort and lodge. There are a few riffles as you pass under the green bridge.

About 0.8 mile downstream from the Cedar Island Estate, and after a large pool, the river narrows to only about 15 feet. The river will push through the Class 1–2 Falls Rapids. The left bank is your best bet to check them out before you run OR to portage. There are a few boulders that you should watch for left of center.

Immediately after Falls Rapids comes the Class 1 Big Twin Rapids. There is some killer wave action as you exit the end of the lake. Scout for deadfall before you run these.

Lying between Sucker Lake and Big Lake are the Class 1 Little Twin Rapids, which are largely composed of riffles.

When you have reached the other end of Big Lake, the Bois Brule will bend to the right and then back left and then enter Class 1 Wildcat Rapids. Stay in the main channel (river-left) past the little island and the rapids will spit you out at Lucius Lake. The relatively short distance covered by these rapids will drop by an impressive 10 feet!

At 2 miles after the outlet of Wildcat, there will be a little S-curve with riffles throughout. Scout for strainers as you proceed.

Only 0.5 mile farther down the road, Winneboujou Landing will appear river-left after a long and winding S-Curve.

Put-in: Stone Bridge. Head south from Brule on WI-27 S for 10 miles. Turn right onto County Road S, and after you cross the river, the put-in will be on the right. *http://goo.gl/maps/V2o7q*

Takeout: Winneboujou Landing. The landing is about 4 miles south of Brule. Follow WI-27 southbound for 3 miles and turn left to stay with 27, and the landing will be less than 1 mile after the curve.

http://goo.gl/maps/IzSLs

While the river should be good to run anytime between late spring and late summer, check to make sure that the CFS is above 125. Contact the Brule River State Forest at: (715) 372-4866 for more information.

There is a campground farther down the river at Brule River State Forest. It is a 20-site, first-come, first-served campground. There is no running tap water at this campground, but there is a hand pump located at the center of the site. For more information call (715) 372-5678.

♪ The Bois Brule sounds like "Penetration" by The Pyramids to us.

7. Chippewa River: County A Bridge to Highway 8 Landing
Difficulty: **A Cinch**
Distance: 9 miles

The Chippewa is approximately one hour north of Eau Claire. This wide, picturesque river once provided an excellent waterway for logging, but today it provides paddlers of all abilities a peaceful, scenic day rolling through its mostly undeveloped shores.

This is a great river to run in late summer to early fall since it is dam fed. On that note, SUPers should exercise caution if there has been a recent outflow from the Arpin Dam. For more information call WDNR Office at Ladysmith: (715) 532-3911, or visit *http://waterdata.usgs.gov/wi/nwis/uv?05356500* to view current and historical water levels.

For 2 miles following the put-in, paddlers will push through a wide and deep section. When you approach the islands, stay river-right to continue in the main channel.

After another couple of miles, there is a public boat landing that will be river-left in between some islands.

At 1.5 miles past the landing you'll pass the Alder Creek Youth Camp. After passing a footbridge, there will be some riffles until you meet the railroad bridge.

Another leisurely 2 miles will bring you to the confluence of the Thornapple River on river-left. There will be another bridge just past the mouth of the river.

At 0.5 mile past the bridge, the Highway 8 Landing will be river-left in between a number of small islands.

Put-in: The County A Bridge put-in is 10 minutes north of Bruce. Make like a baby and "head out" on WI-40 N and then turn right onto Imalone Road. The launch is at the bridge. *http://goo.gl/maps/xlvEp*

Take-out: The Highway 8 Landing is, you guessed it, at the Highway 8 Bridge on the east side of Bruce. *http://goo.gl/maps/S3Aqv*

♪ The Chippewa sounds like "California Sun" by The Rivieras to us.

8. Flambeau River: North Fork/9 Mile to Dix Dox
Difficulty: **Easy—With 1 tight patch**
Distance: 11 miles

The Flambeau slices through the massive and wild 90,000-acre Flambeau River State Forest. Spending a day or two out on the North Fork with your paddleboard will revive your senses. This is one of Wisconsin's largest and least developed public use areas.

The section we recommend is from 9 Mile Landing to Dix Dox. It is slow, wide, and a pitch-perfect harmony to the song your board will be singing once it hits the water.

If you have a buddy following with a canoe, there are some excellent campgrounds along the riverway. Campsites are first-come, first-served, free, and limited to one night only. This 11-mile trip lends itself to an overnighter. Please do not bring any glass onto this river. It is prohibited within the forest.

The Flambeau is good to go during late spring, all summer, and into early fall. In early spring, the snowmelt can create very high water, so caution is advised. The USGS does not maintain a gauge here, so there are no min/max CFS guidelines. Call Flambeau River State Forest for more information: (715) 332-5271.

Put in at 9 Mile Landing and stick to the main channel for the first 2.5 miles as you wind through the scattered boulders and shallow water close to both shores.

About 1 mile past where you see Le Tourneau Creek enter from river-left, you will encounter the Class 1 Barnaby Rapids. The rapids consist of two distinct sets of boulder gardens. These are not dangerous by any means, but it is good practice to eddy out and scout them before choosing your attack.

Another mile down river from the rapids, Butternut Creek enters the river from the right and you will encounter a few small islands.

Just after a pair of islands, the river will fork. Stay right to continue your soul session or left to exit at Deadman's Slough. After passing the landing, you will be joined by Highway 70 for approximately 1 mile.

About 1.5 miles downstream from the landing is the first of two campsites on this route. The County Line Camp is on the left bank, (and word to the wise) the site to the north is much more exposed to sun and wind.

At 3 miles down from County Line Camp, the river will take a sharp left. The three-site Pine Creek Camp is on the left, just past where the Pine Creek enters the river on the right.

At 2 miles after the last campsites, Dix Dox will appear after a narrow island. It is clearly marked with a sign.

Put-in: 9 Mile Landing is 1.5 hours west of Tomahawk, Wisconsin. Leave town on County Road A for 3 miles and turn left onto US-8 W. Follow 8 for 30 miles and exit onto WI-13 N/WI-13 Trunk N toward Ashland. Stay on WI-13 for 30 miles and then turn left onto WI-70 W. After 10 miles, the landing will be on your left. There is also a tavern and canoe rental shop at the launch. The 9 Mile Tavern can be reached at (715) 762-3174. *http://goo.gl/maps/08lux*

Take-out: Dix Dox Landing. Beginning at 9 Mile Landing, head southwest on WI-70/WI-70 Trunk W for 6 miles. Turn right onto Oxbo Drive and then right again onto Dix Dox Road. *http://goo.gl/maps/VGaMs*

The Flambeau sounds like "Bustin' Surfboards" by The Tornadoes to us.

9. Manitowish River: Highway 51 to Highway 47
Difficulty: **Easy Mang**
Distance: 8 miles

Derived from the Ojibwa word for "Spirit People," the Manitowish River seems destined to be a popular river for stand up paddleboarding. The river begins at the outflow of High Lake and then joins the Bear River to create the north fork of the Flambeau. The river moves through marshes and into pine and aspen forests and then once again through open wetland along its 45-mile span. Frequently foggy and misty in the morning, get yourself in the Aloha "spirit" on the Manitowish.

The river is fed from the Rest Lake Dam, so it should generally have enough water for a day out. For more information call the Northern Highland, American Legion State Forest at: (715) 385-2727 or Hawk's Nest Outfitters at: (715) 543-8585

After putting in at the Highway 51 access, you will encounter some low water and rocky riffles. Bring sandals as you may need to hike over or around this situation. After turning to the right, the river will slow and remain so for the rest of the trip.

At 0.75 mile after putting in you will enter Benson Lake. It is ringed with cottages nestled in white and red pines.

About 1.5 miles farther on, you will pass Circle Lily Creek Landing on river-right, just after a left bend in the channel.

After you pass the launch you'll be surfing through bog and open marshland.

At 2 miles downstream from Circle Lily Creek, and after a straight stretch, the river will enter an S-curve where you will see the Highway 51 Wayside Park boat access.

For 0.5 mile beyond the landing, the right bank will have a dramatic and densely treed slope. After the slope fades, the Manitowish becomes an open marsh with grasses and reeds lining the banks. Stay with the main channel as it makes regular sharp turns.

At 3.5 miles past the Wayside Park you will surf under a derelict railroad bridge and then a second bridge serving Highway 47. The Highway 47 take-out is to the right immediately after the bridge.

Put-in: Highway 51 Access. The put-in is about 2 miles from the Manitowish Waters Airport. Head northeast on Airport Road and turn left onto US-51 N/Divine Road. The bridge access will be on the left.

http://goo.gl/maps/kguz3

Take-out: Highway 47 Access. From the put-in, head north on WI-182 E/WI-47 N toward US-51 S. Turn right onto US-51 S and continue on for 5 miles.

http://goo.gl/maps/8375d

The Wisconsin DNR maintains 40 free, well-maintained campsites along the length of the Manitowish.

♪ The Manitowish sounds like "My Big Gun Board" by The Rip Chords to us.

10. Namekagon River: Namekagon Dam Landing to County M Landing
Difficulty: **Intermediate to Advanced, or "Barnie"**—
As in **"Rubble"** 'cause if you're a beginner, you're in trouble.
Distance: 7 miles

The Namekagon is another one of the most popular rivers in the state, second only to possibly the St. Croix. It is actually part of the St. Croix National Scenic Riverway and it has been a designated protected area since 1968. The forward thinking and local commitment has paid off. The Namekagon is actually reversing the trend toward development through public/private partnership and stewardship.

The cold water rushing out of the dam underneath Namekagon Lake is a great place to put an SUP in this river. It tightly twists and turns around islands and through bogs, marshes, and lowland forests. After you've gotten your sea legs on some quieter rivers, let's make it one of the most popular SUP sessions in Wisconsin. Ready to have a blast?

Run this river in late spring and early summer. If you go too far past May or June, then your day out could feel more like a hike than a Stand Up session.

The section we recommend oscillates between wide and quiet to riffles and narrow rushing (easy-ish) rapids. The rapids are largely unnamed and pose little threat. However, it is always good practice to eddy out and plan your attack before charging ahead.

Put in at the inspiringly kept Namekagon Dam Landing on the east side of the road just north of the bridge. After a meandering mile, you'll pass through riffles and boulder gardens that surround a low footbridge.

At 1.5 miles past the footbridge, the Class 1 rapids begin in earnest and they don't stop until close to the County M Landing. At this spot the river narrows and shoots through several hundred yards of rocky, rushing rapids. The rapids finally come to rest in a wide pool. No shame in hiking every once in a while, brothers and sisters!

At 0.5 mile past the rapids, there will be a low logging bridge crossing the river. Another 0.5 mile brings you to another set of rapids. The river narrows and rushes into a long stretch of rapids, which run through a left turn, spilling out into a small pool where a creek enters from river-left.

At 1 mile past the last set of rapids, you encounter the only named set of rapids on this section. Stoll Rapids offer several pitches over about a mile. In medium to high water they can be fun, rolling and wavy, but in low water the rocky bottom and large number of boulders become exposed and can be difficult to surf through. Take-out is at the County M Landing. The hand-carry landing will be river right, just after a left bend and above the bridge.

Put-in: Namekagon Dam. The put-in is 40 miles south of

Ashland. Head out of town on US-2 W for 6 miles and hang a Lucy (left) onto US-63 S. Follow 63 for 13.5 miles and then take a left onto County Highway D. After 9 miles on D, turn right onto Pioneer Road and then left on Crystal Lake Road. After 2 miles, Turn onto Dam Road. *http://goo.gl/maps/fxif0*

Take-out: County M Landing. From the dam, head south on Dam Road for a 1.5 miles. Take a left onto County M and continue for 3.5 miles. The destination will be on the right. *http://goo.gl/maps/aVjTn*

No glass is allowed on this river at any time.

Easier Option: If you would like a more chilled-out trip on this river, consider putting in at Phillipi and taking out at the Cable Wayside.

The National Park Service operates the Namekagon Visitor Center in Trego, Wisconsin. For more information contact them at: (715) 635-8346.

♪ The Namekagon sounds like "Kame-Kaze" by The Challengers to us.

11. St. Croix River: Riverside Landing to Yellow River Landing
Difficulty: **Just like fudge—mostly sweet, but always a little nutty**
Distance: 8.5 miles

The St. Croix is easily the most popular paddle in Wisconsin, if not the whole Midwest, for those sitting-down boater types. Why don't you cut the shuck and jive and see what keeps the St. Croix scene alive. Close to both nature and the Twin Cities, this beautiful river will keep you coming back week after week and year after year.

The creation of the St. Croix National Scenic Riverway in 1968 halted much of the development along the banks of both the Minnesota and Wisconsin side. Dive in and soak up the solitude in the St. Croix's lush garden corridor.

Run this river in the spring through early summer. In mid- to late summer the water will get low enough that you wouldn't have much of a fin left after you were done. Minimum water level is around 125 CFS. Call the National Park Service Namekagon Visitor Center at (715) 635-8346 for more information.

We recommend running the St. Croix from Riverside to Yellow Landing. This slow and spacious section runs though dense forests and is perfect for SUPers of many skill levels. Spend time navigating the many islands and exploring the numerous varied channels.

Put in at the popular Riverside Landing north of the Highway 35 Bridge. Paddle smoothly past the steep, wooded banks and check out the rocky riverbed through the super clear waters.

Look out for the two islands named Hen and Chicken, respectively, which caused loggers of a bygone era regular headaches. They will be just past where Chase Creek enters from river-right.

At 2 miles from Chase Creek, the St. Croix enters the Class 1 Stateline Rapids. Look out for a few little islands before the much larger Ginger Island, where the riffles begin. Caution: in higher water, these can feel a lot more like a Class 2. Only attempt these rapids after you have scouted them and if you feel absolutely comfortable running them.

At 1.5 miles beyond the Stateline Rapids, the Upper Tamarack River will join the St. Croix. A small island sits river-right at the confluence. Beyond the spot that the Upper Tamarack joins, there are a number of islands littered around the remaining stretch.

There are two more creeks that join the river before the landing. Trout Brook and Crystal Creek both enter river-right.

At +2 miles past Crystal Creek there will be a long right curve with three islands. The first two will be smaller than the third. The Yellow River Landing will be river-left near a number of homes.

The St. Croix has over 45 riverside camping sites. Some are right at the put-in at Riverside Landing. For more information contact the St. Croix National Scenic Riverway at: (715) 635-8346.

Put-In: Riverside Landing is about 30 minutes east of I-35 at Hinckley, Minnesota. Exit I-35 and head east on MN-48 for 23 miles. Once back in Wisconsin, continue on WI-77 E for 4 miles and turn left onto WI-35 N/WI-77 E for 8 miles. The landing will be on the right.

http://goo.gl/maps/n18TM

Take-Out: Yellow River Landing. From the put-in at Riverside Landing, head south on WI-35 and take a sharp right onto W. Reservation Road. After 7.2 miles, the Yellow River Landing will be on the left.

http://goo.gl/maps/Fep2E

♪ The St. Croix sounds like "Surf Jam" by The Beach Boys to our ears.

NW Third Coast

12. Apostle Islands

The Apostle Islands are sometimes called the jewels in the crown of Wisconsin. Beautiful is a word that gets thrown around a lot, but this place might have helped define it. Paddle past rising bluffs, incredibly colorful sea caves, and historic lighthouses. The Apostle Islands National Lakeshore is a 21 island archipelago

near the Bayfield Peninsula in pristine Lake Superior. This is one outing not to be missed. It has some of the best water views and routes anywhere, period.

Days out on Lake Superior can be fun and rewarding, but it is a body of water that demands respect. Take the water seriously and watch the weather. Know your kit and respect your limits.

Head out to Meyers Beach, north of Cornucopia, to explore the Bayfield Sea Caves. These sea caves are a jaw-droppingly wonderful part of the Apostle Islands and they are accessible from the mainland. Bright red sandstone cliffs accented with impossibly green trees plunge into amazingly blue water. Eons of waves and weather have created a magnificent mosaic of arches, chambers, and honeycomb-like tunnels.

We recommend going out with a guide even if you are an expert paddler. The water can take a turn for the worse fairly quickly. Contact the Apostle Islands Lakeshore Office for more information: (608) 437-5069. Also consult *http://seacaveswatch. org/* for current wave action.

Put-in: Meyers Beach at the end of Meyer's Road. If you are driving from Bayfield, follow N. 1st Street which becomes WI-13 N/WI-13 Trunk N. Follow 13 for 17 miles and take a right onto Meyers Road/Park Road.

http://goo.gl/maps/gEqdf

Take your SUP out on an overnight camping trip to Oak or Stockton Islands. After setting up camp, explore the spectacular island coast on your paddleboard before tucking in for the night. We recommend these islands because if the wind is too strong to SUP during your visit, there are 11 and 14 miles, respectively, of hiking trails.

Weather and wind permitting, check out the cliffs on the north coast of Oak. They are the highest cliffs on Wisconsin's Superior shoreline. There are also a number of decent beaches to put in at or around.

Also be sure to scope out the Hole-In-The-Wall, which is a beautiful sea arch on the island's northeast side.

On Stockton Island score a campsite right next to your stand up paddling playground of a waterfront at Presque Isle Bay.

A National Park Service permit to camp is required. Apostle Island Cruises offers a shuttle to and from either island. Shuttle cost is $54 per person for the round trip. For more information call Apostle Islands National Lakeshore at (715) 779-3397.

There are a number of local canoe and kayak guides that may be willing to show you around even if you're on an SUP. Call one of them up and you'll be sure to have an excellent trip. Here are a few National Park Service approved guides:

Lost Creek Adventures (715) 209-6956, offering SUP instruction, rentals, and tours of Roman's Point.

Adventure Vacations: (715) 747-2100

Chequamegon Adventure Company: (715) 356-1618

Living Adventure: (715) 779-9503

Trek and Trail: (715) 779-3595

♪ The Apostle Islands sound like "In-Liner" by Dick Dale to us.

13. Chequamegon Bay

The oft mispronounced Chequamegon "she-WAH-meh-gan" Bay is a 12-mile-long inlet of Lake Superior located in the far north of Wisconsin. The name is derived from the Ojibwe word for "place of the sand bars." The Aloha spirit of SUP is really taking hold in many spots along the bay. Check out the Tom

Blade Board Across the Bay Festival in Washburn, enjoy the breathtaking sea caves near Bayfield, or just push off into the bright blue water on a calm day.

Ashland

http://goo.gl/maps/uOf7u

Once a major port and wealthy logging city, the 8,500-person town of Ashland has withstood the test of time and the economic challenges that came with it. Now undergoing a renaissance of a kind, head to this historic, mural-strewn town for a little SUP action.

Start off by visiting Solstice Outdoors to get the scuttlebutt on the sweet spots and rent a board and get gliding! They offer daily and weekly rentals. For more information call: (715) 682-3590

After a day on the water, hit up the Northern Great Lakes Visitor Center, on Highway G, to learn about the history of the area. Then pop over to the South Shore Brewery and Deep Water Grille on W. Main Street for some craft brews and grub.

Maslowski Park has a shallow, sandy swimming beach, playground, pavilion, bathrooms, and an artesian well. There is also access to Ashland's

Lake Front Trail along Chequamegon Bay.
http://goo.gl/maps/i6LW4
    ♪ Ashland sounds like "Surfin' And Spyin'" by The Ventures to us.

Bayfield
http://goo.gl/maps/Shlyt

 Intimately connected to Lake Superior, the charming resort town of Bayfield serves as the gateway to the Apostle Islands and makes for a relaxing base from which to experience all of the SUPing that old Gitchi Gummi has to offer. The town is just far enough away that you will escape the strip-malls, chain stores, and quite possibly your cell signal. Unique Bayfield is home to a not-so-surprisingly vibrant community of outdoor enthusiasts and artisans.

Not that you needed one, but another reason to visit Bayfield is that it was recently awarded the Governor's Tourism

Alex Marks

Stewardship Award and currently holds the record for the most businesses participating in the Travel Green Wisconsin initiative. Although it may be one of Wisconsin's smaller towns, Bayfield is clearly big on sustainability. So why not support a community that is doing it right?

SUPs are available to rent from Superior Adventures on Broad Street. Call (920) 602-0546 for more information. There is a small beach in the heart of town that you could dink around near, or you could head out to Bayview Beach. Head south on Highway 13 for a couple of miles and push out into the wide and shallow beach area. During the summer, this shallow area will be one of the warmest spots around.

Scenic and secluded Little Sand Bay is 15 minutes north of town on Highway 13. The diminutive town of Russell operates a campground, boat launch, picnic area, and a beautiful sand swimming beach. It makes for a fine base for those who are more inclined to explore the area via tent camping. Campsites are $25 a night and a reservation will set you back a fiver. Call them at: (715) 779-5233 for more information. Turn left onto Little Sand Bay Road from Highway 13, the road will end at the campground. *http://goo.gl/maps/3kzMI*

Bark Bay Slough is a great place to work it out on windy days. The labyrinth of channels and islets near the mouth of Lake Superior will not disappoint. The 500-acre natural area is never more than 7 feet deep. Keep an eye peeled for the unique carnivorous plants. Leave town on Front Street/WI-13 N for 25 miles and turn right at Bark Bay Road. *http://goo.gl/maps/PdHAH*

When the surf and sun generate a whopper of an appetite, head to Maggie's Restaurant to try out their Whitefish Livers (!) and Wild Rice. Now that I'm thinking of it, better add the Garlic Polenta Fries to that list as well!

If you are around in October, make sure to add the renowned Apple Festival to your list. For over fifty years, Bayfield has celebrated the harvest with what *Wisconsin Trails Magazine* dubs the "Best Festival in Wisconsin."

♪ Bayfield sounds like "Toes On The Nose" by Eddie & The Showmen to us.

Madeline Island
http://goo.gl/maps/e2k20

 Deflate your board and jump on the car ferry in Bayfield over to wonderful Madeline Island. We've been to many islands in the Midwest (there are more than you might think) and few, if any, hold a candle to Madeline. Stepping off the boat onto this 14-mile-long and 3-mile-wide island is like leaving the cares of the world behind.

Alex Marks

Slow down a little and let yourself be "irie mon." The car ferry takes about 25 minutes and puts you down in the little village of La Pointe. There are shops, restaurants, museums, lodging, trails, grocery stores, coffee, and bike, moped, and kayak rentals all within easy walking distance.

For more information about the ferry, call the Madeline Island Ferry Line at (715) 747-2051.

Apostle Islands Kayaks rents SUPs by the hour for use at their in-town location. Call (715) 747-3636 for more information. They are located close to Joni's Beach. Another option in La Pointe is to rent from Adventure Vacations as well. They can be reached at (715) 747-2100.

Big Bay State Park and Big Bay Town Park are located at opposite ends of Big Bay, which is on the east side of the island. Both parks are located approximately 7 miles from downtown La Pointe. Drive or scoot to one, bearing in mind that the State Park has an entrance fee.

Big Bay State Park has overnight camping and a 1.5-mile-long beach—you guessed it—called Big Bay Beach, listed as one of America's "Top Secret Beaches" by *Budget Travel Magazine* in 2011. There is no launch at the beach, but the hand-carry is manageable. For more information call (888) 947-2757.

Big Bay Town Park also has camping, an idyllic beach, and the added SUPing of the Big Bay Lagoon. There is a long staircase to the beach. Direct queries to (715) 747-2801.

After a long day exploring the coastline of the island, head down to Tom's Burned Down Café. The haphazard collection of stuff that attempts to shelter live music and the always eclectic crowd is reason enough to stop in. Hey, You Gotta Be Tough If You're Gonna Be Dumb!

♪ Madeline Island sounds like "No Waves" by Floating Action to us.

Washburn

http://goo.gl/maps/ar2vu

Tucked next to the shores of Lake Superior, Washburn pushes back the Chequamegon National Forest enough for visitors to enjoy the progressive atmosphere of this vibrant community. At just over 2,000 people, Washburn makes for a good place to SUP.

Check in with Dog Paddle Kayaks at (715) 373-2675 to rent an SUP and then head down to Coal Dock Beach. From Bayfield head north until you come to the Time Out Restaurant. Take a right and head down toward the marina and the Coal Dock is on the left.

Saunter over to Thomson's West End Park for a beach, boat launch, and 27 acres of shoreline access. Camping at the park affords you night views of Ashland's twinkling lights. Sites are occupied on a first-come, first-served basis. For more information call the city office at (715) 373-6160.

Surf pioneer Tom Blake was raised here and there is now an SUP festival and race in his honor. He is credited with fun-

Alex Marks

damental surf innovations such as the fin and hollow board. In late July the Tom Blake Board Across the Bay Race and Festival includes three grueling stand up paddleboard races. There is a 17-mile race across Chequamegon Bay to Ashland and back, an 8.5-mile race and a 1-mile sprint race. There are also equipment demos, instructional clinics, a Saturday evening Hawaiian-themed dinner, and prizes. Visit: *https://sites.google.com/site/tomblakefestival/* for more information.

♪ Washburn sounds like "Noble Surfer" by The Beach Boys to us. Go Tom Blake!

Aaron Peterson/aaronpeterson.net

Surfing Safaris

Here is some food for thought as you plan your SUP attack. Maybe you want to get out in nature, maybe you want to have fun while living it up in the city, and maybe you're so hooked that you want to do it all! Whichever it might be, here are a few itineraries to get you thinking.

City Beaches—2 days—Wicked Weekend

On the first morning, hit Racine's North Beach and then press on to Milwaukee's Bradford Beach. Consider spending the night in Milwaukee at the County Claire Irish Inn and Pub, which is a mere 1.5 miles from the beach. Head north to Kohler Andrea on day two while en route to Sheboygan's Deland Park. Stay overnight in Sheboygan at the GrandStay Residential Suites Hotel.

Endless Summer—7 days—Madison to Madison

Begin day one pushing around Lake Monona and set off to the Dells to hit peaceful Mirror Lake. Stay overnight in the Dells and then continue up to the Castle Rock Flowage for the second day. Camp out at Buckhorn Barrens for an unbelievable sunset. Wake up early and head up north to Bayfield and catch a ferry over to Madeline Island. Knock around the beautiful coastline on Madeline for the remainder of day three. After a dawn patrol on Madeline the next morning, catch the ferry back to the mainland and head down to the Cable area for Day 4. Namekagon Lake and Owen Lake are well situated for some SUP fun. After a fun day four, head southwest for an afternoon out on the sloughs of the mighty Mississippi. Are you tired yet? How could you be when you have a full day of paddling on the Lower Wisconsin ahead of you? Wake up on day seven and head back to the calm waters of Lake Mendota. Whew! That's a busy week off.

Swank Splurge—2 days—Southern (WI) Hospitality

Wisconsin's best water AND hippest hotels go together like stand up and paddling. On day one, hit both Lake Wingra and Mendota and then get as modern as Madison gets at HotelRED in the evening. After waking up in regal splendor, paddle out on Rock Lake en route to Milwaukee's awesome Water Trails and live it up at the iconic Iron Horse Hotel overnight.

Appendix

Yahara Waterways Water Trail Guide

The Yahara Waterways Water Trail Guide is based on *Tay-chopera: A Canoe Guide to Dane County's 4 Lakes* developed in 1984 by the Dane County Environmental Council with text written by Jane Licht. Taychopera means "four lakes" in the Ho Chunk tongue. Taychopera is the glacial-formed chain of lakes, marshes, and river now known as Mendota, Monona, Waubesa, Kegonsa, Upper and Lower Mud, and the Yahara River.

The Yahara Waterways project has been a labor of love for many people. This is especially true considering that people volunteering their time have produced this guide. A special thank you and acknowledgment to the following contributors in the development of this 2007 guide:

✦ Dane County Environmental Council for project initiation and oversight
✦ UW-Extension Environmental Resources Center (Bruce Webendorfer and Jeff Strobel) for editorial assistance, graphic design, and map development
✦ Dane County Lakes and Watershed Commission
✦ Key Members of the Yahara Waterways Steering Committee:
  ✧ Mindy Habecker, project coordinator and author, Dane County UW-Extension
  ✧ Robert Beilman, Madison Audubon Society
  ✧ Steve Falter, Capitol Water Trails
  ✧ Terry Hiltz, Wisconsin River Alliance
  ✧ Sue Jones, coordinator, Dane County Lakes and Watershed Commission and Dane County Office of Lakes and Watersheds